Morocco

Morocco

BY ETTAGALE BLAUER
AND JASON LAURÉ

Enchantment of the World
Second Series

A Division of Grolier Publishing

NEW YORK   LONDON   HONG KONG   SYDNEY
DANBURY, CONNECTICUT

Consultant: James A. Winship, Ph.D., Professor of Political Science and William Freistat Professor of Studies in World Peace, Augustana College, Rock Island, Illinois

Please note: All statistics are as up-to-date as possible at the time of publication.

Visit Children's Press on the Internet: http://publishing.grolier.com

Book Production by Herman Adler Design Group
Book Design by Ox and Company

Library of Congress Cataloging-in-Publication Data

Blauer, Ettagale.
    Morocco / by Ettagale Blauer and Jason Lauré.
        p. cm. — (Enchantment of the world. Second series)
    Includes bibliographical references and index.
    Summary: Describes the geography, plants and animals, history, economy, language, religions, culture, and people of Morocco, a unique northern African nation surrounded by both water and desert.
    ISBN 0-516-20961-2
    1. Morocco—Juvenile literature. [1. Morocco.] I. Lauré, Jason.
II. Title. III. Series.
DT305.B53 1999
916.4—dc21   98-17644
                                                                      CIP
                                                                       AC

Acknowledgments

Through our many visits to Morocco we have relied on the Moroccan people to guide us through their country and their cultures. We gratefully acknowledge the insights provided to us by Del Blaoui. We thank Bashara Blaoui for the long discussions we had about life in Morocco today. We are extremely thankful to Mohammed Fikri, who permitted us to attend his wedding in Meknes, and to Nezha Mestour, sister of the bride, who invited us to the bride's party in Fez. Everywhere along the way we were helped by Moroccans who shared their feelings about their country and their hopes for its future.

Cover photo:
A Berber girl

Contents

An artisan at work

Riding a "ship of the desert"

Crossroads of Cultures

Snow-capped mountains, beaches, oceans and deserts! There is no country like Morocco. It occupies a unique place in the geography of Africa as well as in the world of cultures. It is at once African, French, Spanish, Arabic, Berber, and Muslim. It embraces ancient sites and cultures as well as modern cities.

K ING HASSAN II SAYS MOROCCO IS "ROOTED IN Africa, watered by Islam and rustled by the winds of Europe." Some of Morocco's citizens have roots that stretch back a thousand years. It is a country with one official religion, Islam, yet it has always been tolerant of other religions. In a region where Islamic extremists try to direct every move of the people, Morocco is relaxed about the practice of its official religion. Morocco's official language is Arabic, but French

Opposite: **Mountains tower behind the city of Marrakesh.**

Roman ruins at Volubilis

is widely spoken in business and government and is taught in school.

Morocco is African because it is located at the northwest corner of the African continent. Yet black Africans aren't native to Morocco. The population is divided into two main language groups— Arabic speakers and Berbers, the people who lived in Morocco long before the Arabs and Europeans arrived. Even though they speak different languages and have different cultures, they are all Muslims—people who follow the Islamic religion.

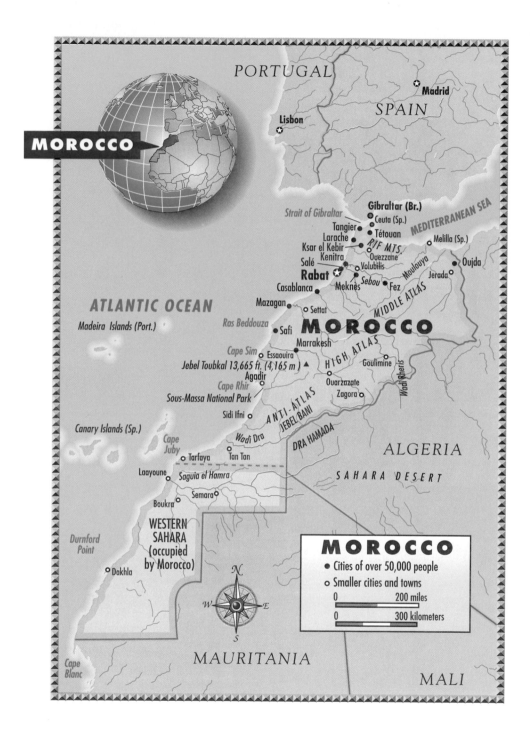

PORTUGAL

SPAIN

★ **Madrid**

Lisbon ✪

Gibraltar (Br.)
Strait of Gibraltar
Ceuta (Sp.)
Tangier
Tétouan
Larache
RIF MTS.
Ksar el Kebir
Melilla (Sp.)
Kenitra
Ouezzane
Oujda
Salé
Volubilis
Jerada
Rabat ★
Sebou
Meknès   Fez
Casablanca
Mazagan
MIDDLE ATLAS
Settat
Mouloya

ATLANTIC OCEAN

Ras Beddouza
MOROCCO
Safi
Madeira Islands (Port.)
Marrakesh
Cape Sim
Essaouira   HIGH ATLAS
Goulimine
Jebel Toubkal 13,665 ft. (4,165 m) ▲
Wadi Rheris
Agadir
Ouarzazate
Cape Rhir
Zagora
Sous-Massa National Park
ANTI-ATLAS
Sidi Ifni
JEBEL BANI

Canary Islands (Sp.)
Wadi Dra
DRA HAMADA
Cape Juby
ALGERIA
Tarfaya   Tan Tan
Laayoune
SAHARA DESERT
Saguia el Hamra
Semara

Durnford Point
WESTERN
SAHARA
(occupied
by Morocco)
Dakhla

N
W   E
S

MOROCCO
● Cities of over 50,000 people
○ Smaller cities and towns
0   200 miles
0   300 kilometers

MAURITANIA

MALI

Cape Blanc

Geopolitical map
of Morocco

Looking to Europe

Morocco was considered part of the Maghreb, the region of North Africa that stretches eastward through Algeria, Tunisia, and parts of Libya. This makes it an Arab nation. Yet many Moroccans spend most of their lives working in the countries of Europe where Muslims and Arabs are in the minority. Their own country cannot create enough jobs to allow them to remain at home. Much of the money they earn abroad is sent back to relatives in Morocco and is an important part of the Moroccan economy. Europe is so close to Morocco, it is possible to stand on the shore at Tangier and look across the Strait of Gibraltar and see Spain. It's just 8 1/2 miles (13.6 km) away, across the Mediterranean Sea. More than 1.5 million Moroccans work in Europe. Many of them come home in the summer for their annual vacation.

Berber men with their camels in the south of Morocco

Morocco is unique because it is surrounded by vast bodies of water—the Atlantic Ocean and the Mediterranean Sea—and a huge, trackless desert—the Sahara. Great mountain ranges slice across the nation, dividing it into regions that are very separate from one another. Travel is extremely difficult. These mountains also give the country a climate that changes abruptly with the altitude. Modern transportation, including airplanes and automobiles, serves part of the population while others still rely on camels and donkeys to take them to market. All these geographical features make Morocco seem more like an island. They isolate the country from its African neighbors.

King Hassan II greets crowds as he arrives at the royal palace.

Ruled by a King

Morocco is one of the few nations still ruled by a king. His name is Hassan II and he is the son of Mohammed V, the first king to rule Morocco after independence. Hassan II is one of the last kings in Africa, and he has virtually complete control over the people. Morocco also has an emerging democratic form of government. The people vote for the members of Parliament. Morocco seems to have been most successful in dealing with its colonial past. It was one of the first African nations to gain its independence, yet it did so only after sending thousands of its men to fight on the side of France, its colonial master. Even its colonial period was unique. Morocco was divided into two regions by France and Spain, and different parts were ruled by each of those two countries.

Morocco is unique because King Mohammed V gave the people their own identity, one that was separate from both the French and the Spanish. He was able to unite all the people into fighting for independence and resisting the French who ruled Morocco. His personal bravery made him a symbol of the people's determination and made him even more popular and important to the nation after it gained its independence.

Morocco is unique because its ancient Islamic heritage is part of everyday life in its great cities. It's visible in the ancient buildings and walled cities that make it an appealing and friendly destination for tourists. It has a remarkable ability to absorb hundreds of thousands of foreigners each year. Visitors come to see the ancient, imperial cities. They hope to find the romantic atmosphere depicted in the

The modern city of Casablanca

movie *Casablanca*. Though that exotic city is nowhere to be found in the real Casablanca, visitors find all they could have hoped for and more in Morocco's walled cities, teeming markets, and 2,000-year-old historic sites.

In every way, Morocco is a unique nation.

Mountains, Desert, and Sea

Dramatic contrasts mark every part of Morocco's territory. These contrasts help to determine how and where the people live. The beauty of the country is found in a variety of terrain including beaches, mountains, and desert. But these same beautiful regions also present very difficult living conditions. Temperatures rise and fall abruptly when the sun comes up and goes down.

MOROCCO WAS ONCE DESCRIBED as a "cold country with a hot sun." Its beauty has inspired the artists and writers who have made Morocco their second home. When the great French painter Eugène Delacroix traveled through Morocco for six months in 1832, he was enchanted by the sights that greeted him, especially the Arabs and their horses, the quality of the light, and the sense of an ancient people. American author Paul Bowles lived in Tangier for more than thirty years. In his novels, including *The Sheltering Sky, Let It Come Down*, and *The Spider's House*, he explores the problems of Westerners who find themselves trying to live in an Eastern, or oriental, world.

A Moroccan Saddling a Horse, **by Eugène Delacroix**

British Prime Minister Winston Churchill, who led his country during World War II, discovered Morocco on his visit there to meet with U.S. President Franklin Delano Roosevelt. Churchill frequently returned to Marrakesh after he retired from political life. He made his base at the elegant Hotel La Mamounia in Marrakesh, where he painted landscapes.

Morocco is bordered by the Mediterranean Sea on the north and the Atlantic Ocean on the west. To the east lies the country of Algeria. The southern border of the country is not

Opposite: **A valley in the High Atlas mountain range**

Geographical Features

Highest Elevation: Jebel Toubkal, 13,671 feet (4,167 m)

Lowest Elevation: Sebkha Tah, 180 feet (55 m) below sea level

Average Temperatures: High, 64–82° F (18–28°C); Low, 46–63°F (8–17°C)

Location with Highest Average Temperature: Interior regions in summer

Location with Lowest Average Temperature: Atlas Mountains

Longest River: Moulouya, 320 miles (515 km) long, drains to the Mediterranean

Largest City: Casablanca

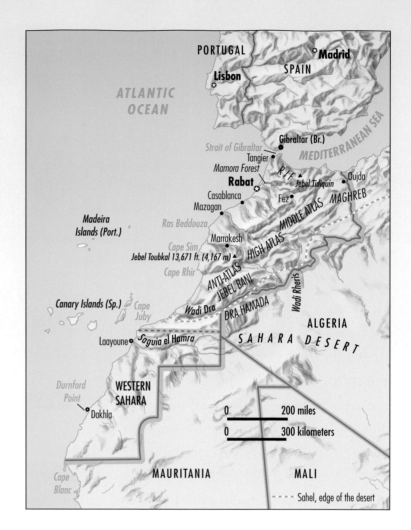

The Maghreb

Maghreb is an Arabic word that means "the place of sunset, the west." It describes a section of North Africa that begins in Morocco and extends eastward through Algeria, Tunisia, and the northwestern portion of Libya. It is a term that includes the region's geography as well as its political and cultural aspects. Originally, it was used to explain the two parts of the Islamic world—the western part and the eastern part, which includes the Islamic countries of the Middle East.

Today, the greatest differences may be found in countries that exist side by side, such as Morocco and its neighbor Algeria. While Morocco is a country where both the local citizens and foreign visitors feel comfortable, Algeria is going through a kind of civil war, and foreigners are advised to stay away. Relations between the countries are very tense because Algeria supported a political group called the Polisario in its war against Morocco to gain control of the Western Sahara.

firmly settled. Morocco claims the area formerly known as the Spanish Sahara, which was ruled by Spain from 1904 to 1975. Although the rest of the world calls this region the Western Sahara, Morocco simply calls it the south of Morocco and considers its southern border to be the country of Mauritania. Morocco's total land area is 274,152 square miles (710,000 sq km). Western Sahara represents one-third of that total, or 101,823 square miles (263,700 sq km).

Mountains of Morocco

Four mountain ranges stretch across Morocco, acting as barriers to travel and to communication. They also serve to separate the two major population groups, the Arabs and the Berbers. The mountains run roughly in the same direction as the country itself, from the northeast to the southwest. The northernmost range is called the Rif. The Rif Mountains rise up steeply from the Mediterranean and then follow the coastline from east to west. The highest peak of the Rif, Jebel Tidiquin, is an imposing mountain of 8,056 feet (2,455 m). The Rif forms a great barrier that protects the cities on the Mediterranean coast, especially Tangier, from the harsh and drying winds of the south.

Atlas Mountains

Farther south, fertile plains separate the Rif Mountains from the next range, known as the Middle Atlas. This range covers the country from just south of the Rif and runs to the southwest into the midsection of the country. The Middle Atlas nearly overlaps the High Atlas, the highest range in the coun-

Casablanca

Casablanca is Morocco's largest city, with a population of 3,210,000 (1990 estimate, greater city). The city's ethnic groups include Arab-Berber, Jewish, European, and others. The city was founded in the twelfth century. Portuguese settlers arrived in 1515. After a huge earthquake in the late 1700s, the city was rebuilt.

Located on the Atlantic coast, Casablanca is Morocco's most active port. Its altitude is 164 feet (50 m) above sea level. In January, the average temperature is 60°F (16°C). In July, the average temperature is 72°F (22°C). The city's important landmarks include the *medina*, or site of the old city; the Grand Mosque; and the Mosque Hassan II.

try. The High Atlas forms a virtual wall across the country, stretching from the Atlantic coast to the northeast for 430 miles (692 km). The mountains reach their high point of 13,671 feet (4,167 meters) at Jebel Toubkal, the highest peak in all of North Africa. For spectacular views, visitors can climb Jebel Toubkal. From April to November, daytime temperatures are pleasant. Between December and March, however, the upper slopes are covered with ice and snow.

The High Atlas forms the most dramatic barrier of all the mountain ranges in Morocco. On the northern side, the mountains are dotted with streams, woods, and valleys. On the southern slopes, the mountains look to the Sahara. The

Jebel Toubkal is the highest peak in North Africa.

High Atlas also divides the country into two major zones of climate. To the north of the range, the country receives the cool winds of the Atlantic Ocean, while to the south, the hot drying air of the Sahara is the dominant force.

The mountain ranges occupy much of Morocco's land. More than 38,613 square miles (100,000 sq km) of the land is covered by mountain peaks at least 6,562 feet (2,000 m) high. The people who live in these areas are isolated for most of the year, either by the weather or by the difficulty of traveling even small distances. More than a dozen peaks are higher than 13,123 feet (4,000 m).

The fourth range, known as the Anti-Atlas, actually touches the High Atlas at one end. At the other, it runs to the

Marrakesh

Marrakesh, located in the foothills of the Atlas Mountains, has a population of 1,517,000 (1990 estimate, greater city). The city's largest ethnic group is Arab-Berber (99.1%), with Jews (0.2%), and Europeans and others (0.07 %). The city was founded in 1062 by Yusuf ibn Tashufin of the Almoravid dynasty.

The city has an altitude of 1,541 feet (470 m). In January, the average daily temperature is 50°F (10°C). In July, the average daily temperature is 82°F (28°C). Marrakesh is one of the great Islamic cities of North Africa. Important landmarks include the twelfth-century Koutoubia Mosque, Djemaa el Fna, the medina, the sultan's palace and gardens, and the royal tombs.

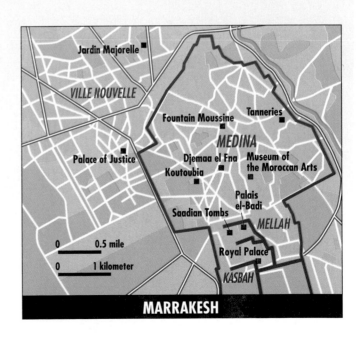

Atlantic coast. After the Anti-Atlas, there is little but the harsh landscape of the Western Sahara. The word *sahara* means "desert" in Arabic. From here, the Atlantic coastline is a wild and rugged stretch with cliffs that drop off sharply to the icy waters below. Virtually all of the Sahara region is bleak desert land with almost no water. It offers few resources to support permanent settlements.

Valleys and Lowlands

A fisher tries his luck in the rough waters of the Atlantic Ocean.

Between these mountain ranges lie valleys and lowlands. The Sous River Valley lies between the High Atlas and the Anti-Atlas. A vast plateau, ranging in height from 1,772 to 2,953 feet (540 to 900 m), covers the interior of the country. Although this region has poor soil, it includes the area of Khouribga, also known as the phosphates plateau. Two other regions are better suited for agriculture—the Tadla Plain, on the Oum er Rbia River, and the Haouz, on the Tensift River. Morocco's many rivers are important for irrigation, especially during the frequent periods of drought that affect the country.

Fifty thousand to 100,000 years ago, when Europe was still covered by sheets of ice, the Sahara was a warm and pleasant region with grassy steppes and mountains covered by forests. Rivers wound their way through the region and herds of elephants, rhinos, hippos, giraffes, and zebras found good grazing right up to the edge of the Atlas Mountains.

But when the ice sheets receded about 10,000 years ago, and the climate in Europe became warm enough to support human life, the climate in north Africa changed too. In time,

Wildflowers bloom along the Dra River in spring.

the Sahara region dried out. The plants and the rivers dried out too, and with them went the wildlife. The only remaining evidence that such animals once flourished here can be found in rock paintings in the Atlas Mountains.

While mountain ranges slice through the country's northern section, the Sahara acts as a virtual wall across the south of Morocco. The extreme daytime temperatures can dry out the skin in minutes, yet at night the temperature often drops forty degrees. The land, mostly hard-packed sand, doesn't hold either the cold or the heat, so the traveler is subject to both extremes.

There are no roads through the heart of the Sahara, only trails known by the French word *piste*, which means "track." Pistes are often turned into corrugated ridges of hard-packed sand by the heavily laden

How the Winds Blow

Winds are a crucial factor in Morocco's climate. Each wind has a particular name and occurs in a different season. The *chergui* is a dry wind that blows out of the Sahara from the southwest, bringing hot, burning temperatures. The *gharbi* is a cold, wet wind that blows directly out of the Atlantic Ocean from the west. These winds turn part of the country into beautiful forests while other parts are covered with high, sun-baked sand dunes. On the same day that the Sahara is baking in the sun, parts of the High Atlas are covered with snow. Snowstorms can whip up in the Atlas even on a pleasant April day, while a blinding sandstorm can bring a halt to travel in the Sahara totally without warning.

Tangier

The port of Tangier, the "gateway to Africa," is at least 3,000 years old and was an important trading center more than 2,000 years ago. Its strategic location at the Strait of Gibraltar made it a rich target for anyone wishing to control access to the Mediterranean and the Atlantic Ocean. Tangier was conquered over and over again by the Arabs, the Spanish, and the Portuguese. The town was even "given" as a part of the wedding dowry of Catherine of Braganza, Portugal, when she married Charles II of England in 1661. That left the English in charge of Tangier. They didn't have it for long.

In 1684, the Arabs re-took the city under their leader Moulay Ismail. For more than 200 years the city remained firmly in the hands of the Muslims. Even when Morocco became a French protectorate in 1912, the city of Tangier was not included. Instead, it was declared an "international zone" and was controlled jointly by eight European countries. Tangier was reunited with Morocco at the time of independence, in 1956. It is the most-visited city in Morocco, welcoming 1 million people every year. There is now talk of building a bridge 19 miles (31 km) long from near Tangier across the Strait of Gibraltar to Spain.

The endless dunes of the Sahara

trucks that carry goods to the south and the interior. This surface jolts and jars everything that passes over it, restricting travel to only the hardiest of vehicles and people. One paved road runs along the coastline but it still requires a four-wheel-drive vehicle.

Endless Dunes

Although much of the Sahara is hard-packed sand, 10 percent of the area is covered by vast, shifting sand dunes. These great masses of sand are constantly on the move. The winds ripple

Earthquake!

February 9, 1960, was an end as well as a second beginning for the town of Agadir. On that day, an earthquake struck this ancient port city, which was first settled by Berber fishermen around the twelfth century. In the early sixteenth century, it became a strategic port for the Portuguese. By the mid-sixteenth century, however, the Portuguese had been forced out of Agadir (as well as all their other footholds along the Atlantic coast of Morocco). The 1960 earthquake completely flattened the town, killing 15,000 people and destroying 4,000 buildings. A modern city was built from the rubble of that destruction. Agadir's beach is considered the best in Morocco. Agadir is also the principal port for Morocco's sardine catch.

across the very edge of the dunes and blow grains of sand up one side of the dunes. Then the sand that is blown over the top begins its journey down the other side. In this way the dunes seem to "walk" across the desert.

Although the heat in the desert during the day is extreme, when the sun goes down, the temperature drops rapidly. Because there are no trees or grasses to hold the heat, and no moisture in the soil, the land cools off dramatically. It is typical for the temperature to drop forty degrees at night. The desert extends right to the Atlantic Ocean. A narrow strip of land along the shore has a pleasant—even cool—atmosphere, but take just a short walk inland and the heat is scorching.

Saharan Provinces

The basic shape of a country is not usually a matter of dispute these days, but it is in the case of Morocco. The country's land area was once much greater than it is today, extending deep into the Sahara and including parts of present-day Mali. But by the nineteenth century, Morocco was in control of a much smaller area. Sultans who controlled various parts of the territory fought to maintain their rule. The country's borders were set by about 1880, giving the country a land area about the size of California. At that time, the southern border was the Spanish Sahara, ruled by Spain.

Then, in 1975, King Hassan II ordered his people to march across the border into Spanish Sahara and "reclaim" the territory as part of Morocco. Since then, Moroccan maps show that the country includes the Spanish Sahara, and its southern border is now Mauritania. This increases its land area by nearly one-half and greatly increases the length of its Atlantic Ocean coastline, from 1,140 miles (1,835 km) to 1,802 miles (2,900 km). The United Nations has not recognized Morocco's claims to the region. A local resistance movement, the Polisario, wants the territory to become an independent nation.

Tuaregs gather for a festival in the former Spanish Sahara.

CHAPTER THREE

A Look at Nature

The story of wildlife and plant life in Morocco is one of disappearing resources. The loss of some species is due to changes in climate over hundreds of years. The loss of much of the country's forests is much more recent and can be traced to human activity.

A cedar forest in the
Rif Mountains

Finches still sing in Morocco's
remaining forests.

Opposite: **An oasis pool
near the High Atlas**

THE GREAT FORESTS OF CEDAR TREES THAT ONCE COVERED much of the Atlas Mountains and the Rif Mountains have been greatly reduced. These trees, along with cork oak trees and pistachio trees, have been cut down for cooking and heating fires. Each time village women go out looking for firewood, they must walk farther and carry their heavy loads for longer distances.

The remaining cedar forests still cover about 325,000 acres (131,528 ha). Some of these trees reach a height of 200 feet (61 m) and can be 400 years old. Wherever forests remain, a few animals still live. There may be a dozen leopards still living in the forests. And there is quite a variety of bird life left in the country. In the forests, the songs of small finches and other songbirds may still be heard. Many species of birds migrate to Morocco to spend the winter.

Cork oak trees

Unique Forests

The argan tree is a unique species found in Morocco. It is similar to the olive tree and its fruit is processed for the oil it contains. These hardy trees do well in dry areas where there is a mist that provides enough water for them. Argan trees grow along the lower slopes of the mountain ranges, mainly between the Atlantic coast and the city of Ouarzazate. Goats find the leaves of the argan very tasty, but the leaves are usually too high up to reach. So the goats just climb up the tree trunks and stand on the branches—an amazing sight.

Sous-Massa National Park

Where there is water, there is life. In Sous-Massa National Park, just south of Agadir, a narrow strip surrounding the Sous River gives life to a variety of birds as well as scrubby vegetation. Thanks to the river, this region has the most vegetation and wildlife in the country. The riverbanks attract hundreds of species of migrating birds. Some spend the winter there, while others stop over briefly. They find plenty to eat along the fertile river banks. Perhaps the most impressive are the greater flamingos (below). These pink birds with their pencil-thin legs and elegant necks arrive by the hundreds in winter. They fly south from southern Spain and France. The most distinctive tree in this region is the thorny euphorbia (far right). With its giant cactuslike arms reaching upward, it resembles a huge, upside-down umbrella.

In the region between Rabat, Kenitra, and Meknès lies the Mamora Forest. This unique forest has just one species of tree, the cork oak. When the trees are twenty-seven years old, the outer layers are removed by making a long cut on the trunk and then peeling them off. This can be done only once in about nine years. In between, the tree is left to recover and to grow new outer layers. When the tree is too old for cork, it is used for firewood.

The Desert

Traveling south past the High Atlas Mountains and the cities of Ouarzazate and Er-Rachidia, the Sahara begins to make itself felt. The air grows drier, the vegetation grows sparse, and the landscape is tan-colored. The sky seems enormous and the land seems to stretch out forever. The remains of hundreds of tiny adobe buildings are scattered across the land near the cities. These are known as *kasbahs*, a word we associate with mysterious places and intrigue. But the original kasbahs were

Opposite: **Kasbah ruins**

The Oasis

There are few sights more amazing than a true oasis. After riding for 100 miles (161 km) in the desert, seeing only the beige of the sand, the dazzling blue of the sky, and the intense yellow of the sun, a traveler might think the sight of palm trees was a mirage—an illusion. Those palm trees are a sure sign of an oasis, a place where there is underground water and the possibility of life.

Desert travelers depend on the oases to keep them going across the vast empty stretches of dry land without a tree, a bush, or a bit of green in sight. The natural underground water is hauled to the surface, usually by a pulley and bucket. The power may be supplied by a person or a donkey. Small villages rise from the desert sands. The date palm trees provide fruit and a product to sell. The water is used to grow crops on small bits of land along a narrow section that straddles the water source.

During the drought that hit the region in the early 1990s, many of these centuries-old oases dried up. That drought put an end to the traditional life of the nomadic people who moved with their herds of small animals. Without water, nothing survives. When the rainfall returned, the desert bloomed once again, but it was too late for people who had lost all their sheep, goats, and camels.

forts or any living place that had some kind of fortification. Since there is no wood to build with in these regions, the people used packed earth, baked in the sun. Where there was stone, the kasbahs were made of stone. And wherever there is an oasis, with its underground supply of water, plants are cultivated. The Sahara is a place of such emptiness that the occasional oasis seems like a fairyland. The astonishing sand dunes of the Erg Chebbi dramatically announce the presence of the desert. Some rise to more than 800 feet (244 m).

Ship of the Desert

The camel is a remarkable beast, well suited to desert life. It is called the "ship of the desert" because it can travel across a region that is very much like the ocean. No other animal, and very few vehicles, manage to survive the extremes of heat and cold without a fresh supply of water. The camel can carry a load of 400 pounds (181 kg) or even more. Everything about the camel is designed for life in the desert. Its hump stores fat, and it can survive losing up to 25 percent of its body weight in water through dehydration. Its eyes are protected from sand by heavy lashes and brows. Its padded feet, like snowshoes, are perfect for crossing desert sands and hard-packed desert surfaces. Camels are extremely valuable and very expensive. One camel can cost $1,000. The camel used in Morocco has one hump and is called a dromedary. Camels were brought to the region almost 2,000 years ago by the Romans. They became vital links in the trade routes established across the Sahara. They traveled the classic caravan route, from Marrakesh to Timbuktu.

Desert Caravans

What kind of trade could be so important that men would risk their lives to cross the Sahara on camels? Salt! This simple, everyday item was once the only way to preserve meat, and it was valued by people throughout the world. Caravans were also used to transport goods made in one region and needed in another.

Even in modern times, when droughts occur, caravans set out across the desert. One such caravan came to a campsite near Tiznit one night, and its leader spoke with visitors. He had to find food for his people. To do this, he was going to sell some of his precious camels at the market. He spoke in Arabic and the interpreter spoke in French as he described his journey from northern Ghana through Timbuktu. It had taken him fifty nights to reach this market, he said, traveling at night because the heat was bearable then. It was difficult to part with any of his beloved camels, but by doing so he would bring back enough food to keep his people going until the rains returned. He could not even imagine a place called America. He had only one question to ask his visitors from far away: "Do you have water in your country?"

A camel market

From the Romans to Independence

Morocco has been inhabited for more than 2,000 years with a changing cast of nationalities and languages. Everything about the country today is the continuation of a culture established 1,200 years ago. The various nations that colonized Morocco, or parts of it, have left their mark. Some are true leftovers, bits of land that are still ruled by another nation even though they are part of Morocco's territory. But the most long-lasting influences were those of the Berbers, the Arabs, and the French. The history of Morocco is a history of these waves of migration.

IN THE LATE STONE AGE, SOME 8,000 YEARS AGO, NEOLITHIC people lived along Morocco's Mediterranean coast. Groups that lived south of the mountain range found plenty of game to hunt and crops to support their cattle. They disappeared when the climate began to change, about 6,000 years ago.

Berbers Arrive

The first modern people to arrive were the Berbers, who came from Europe or Asia about 4,000 years ago. Although their origins remain a mystery, it is believed that some of the Berbers migrated from southwestern Asia—present-day Kazakhstan. They were the ancestors of the majority of Morocco's population.

Morocco's geographical position made it the center of a lively trade set up by the Phoenicians. The Berbers were in contact with these traders more than 3,000 years ago. About 1,000 years later, the Carthaginians, who were descendants of the Phoenicians, established a trading post at Tangier. They also built the town of Rabat, now the capital of Morocco.

The Berbers developed kingdoms and controlled vast stretches of land as far south as the Senegal River in present-day Mali. They came under the control of the powerful Roman Empire around A.D. 40.

The people of the Arabian Peninsula, to the east, were converted to Islam in the late 600s A.D. Islam required rulers

Opposite: **Roman ruins of Volubilis**

From the Romans to Independence **37**

Volubilis

Nearly 2,000 years ago, the Romans controlled this part of North Africa. Volubilis was inhabited until the eighteenth century, when the site was stripped of its beautiful marble. It was taken away and used to build palaces for Moulay Ismail in nearby Meknès. Walking around the well-preserved ruins, it's easy to imagine the life of the ancient people who lived there. Mansions and a triumphal arch built by a Roman emperor can be seen. Beautiful mosaic floors depict scenes from mythology as well as important events of the time. These lively pictures in stone are bright and fresh 2,000 years after they were created.

to have religious authority as well as authority over political or civil matters. There was no separation between the state and the religion. The Arabs moved westward across North Africa, bringing Islam with them. They were slowed down, however, when they ran into the Berbers, who are fiercely independent people. Although they eventually conquered the Berbers, the Arabs never really controlled their daily lives. The Berbers continued to follow their own tribal laws, rather than the *sharia*—the laws of Islam.

Chaos followed in Morocco over the next several hundred years. The practice of Islam became confused and strayed far from the original ideals of the religion. The Arabs and the Berbers were in constant conflict until the arrival of the Almoravids. The Almoravids were tough desert people from the land known as Mauritania, in the south. They were led by Youssef ben Tachfin, who created his capital at Marrakesh in 1062. The town began as a fortified camp, a safe place. Youssef conquered Fez and soon controlled the entire North African coast of Morocco, except for certain ports that were held by Spanish Muslims. Youssef also controlled the land of Andalusia in southern Spain.

The Almoravids drew from cultures that they conquered, including the Moorish culture of Spain. It is thought that the Moors were Arabs and Berbers who came from Morocco in the eighth century and conquered Spain. The origin of the word *Moor* is not known; some think it came from the word *Morocco*. The mix of cultures, the borrowing and changing, helped form the period known as the golden age of culture and civilization in Morocco. The Almoravids greatly enlarged the

Kairouyine Mosque and religious university in Fez, built in 859–862. Under Youssef, the cities of Morocco became important centers of power and wealth. His son briefly continued his father's work but soon lost interest in everything but religion. Without a strong leader, Morocco lost much of the land it had gained as well as any sense of a unified nation. In 1147 the Almoravid dynasty was overthrown by the Almohads.

The Kairouyine Mosque in Fez has room for 20,000 people.

Almohad Dynasty

During the next 100 years, the Almohad dynasty held power. The Almohads conquered not only Morocco but also held power over what are now the countries of Algeria, Tunisia, and part of Libya. They also expanded northward into Spain. The influence of Spain's Moorish culture can still be seen in Marrakesh and Rabat. But the power of the Almohads came to a sudden end in the thirteenth century, in part because they spent so much of their energy and resources fighting to keep their lands in Spain. Their North African territory was divided into three parts, today known as Tunisia, Algeria, and

Moulay Idriss

This charming town, set within the mountains, is named after the saint Moulay Idriss, who was a great-grandson of the prophet Muhammad. (*Moulay* is a title of respect. It indicates that the person is a descendant of the prophet.) Moulay Idriss is one of most revered people in Moroccan history. He came to Volubilis from Mecca in the eighth cen-tury and was a key figure in converting people to Islam. He created Morocco in A.D. 788 when he was proclaimed the king. His son, Idriss II, settled in the small town of Fez and made it his capital. Today, Moulay Idriss is a holy site for Muslims. People who are not Muslims may not enter the mosques or stay overnight.

Morocco. Remarkably, the borders established before the fifteenth century are very much the same today.

In the thirteenth century, Morocco came under the control of the Merinids, who ruled for 200 years. They built many of Morocco's religious schools during their dynasty.

Ultimately, this Berber dynasty was unsuccessful because it was unable to unite the many small tribes brought under its rule. Each of these tribes was loyal to its own leader, in its own region. There was no sense of belonging to a nation. When a leader died or lost power, the tribes fought against one another. They were then too weak to resist foreigners who invaded their territory.

The Merinids were losing out in Spain as well. The religious persecution known as the Inquisition threw all Jews and Muslims out of Spain in 1492. The spread of Islam into Spain was not only stopped, it was pushed back to North Africa.

Toledo

Lisbon

Valencia

GRANADA MEDITERRANEAN SEA

Tunis

Rabat (1160)

Tiemcen

Fez (1069) *ZAYANID KINGDOM 1235–1545*

Tinnel

Marrakesh

MERINID KINGDOM 1248–1465

Sijilmasa (1055)

HAFSID KINGDOM 1229–1574

0 200 miles
0 300 kilometers

11th–14th Centuries

Almoravids 1050–1147

- - - Almohads 1125–1220

GRANADA Berber Kingdoms 1229–1574

Violent Times

In the early 1500s, the Portuguese conquered most of the Atlantic coastal towns, but they didn't hold on to them for long. The Saadi tribe began a religious war against the Portuguese and gained control of strategic ports the

Portuguese had held. The Saadian dynasty lasted only 100 years but it was very bloody.

The Alawites (or Alaouites), the next tribe to rule Morocco, created a dynasty that still rules Morocco today. The most important Alawite ruler, Sultan Moulay Ismail, ruled for fifty-five years, from 1672 to 1727. His reign was one of the darkest times in Morocco's history. He was a cruel and ruthless leader who kept hundreds of thousands of slaves. He is known to have killed thousands of people. At the same time, however, he brought the Arabs and the Berbers together as a unified nation. He is also known for building many bridges, ports, roads, and forts during his rule. When he died, he left the country in a desperate state. There was a great revolt among the people he had treated so harshly. The unity he achieved by force quickly fell apart and, once again, Morocco had no one to guide it.

Morocco never really recovered after that. Weak rulers and mounting debts drained the country. These debts led the Moroccans to look outside their own borders for help. In the 1880s, the European nations were intent on their colonial adventures. In Africa, they saw a vast land full of resources. Morocco's weakness made it an easy target for the Europeans, once they stopped fighting among themselves. Four countries got together to divide Morocco—France, Britain, Spain, and Germany. It was almost by chance that Morocco came under French rule. As the European nations traded land back and forth, France acquired most of Morocco—but not all of it.

Spanish Claims

Spain had established a foothold in several regions, including a crescent-shaped section of the northern coast that stretched from Ceuta in the west to Melilla in the east. Spain still holds these two cities today. They are called enclaves because they are surrounded by Morocco. Spain also held two regions on the Atlantic coast—the enclave of Sidi Ifni, and Tarfaya, a territory that stretched across the southernmost part of Morocco all the way to the border of Algeria. Spanish Sahara, an enormous territory south of Tarfaya, was held entirely by the Spanish.

Ceuta is a Spanish enclave on Morocco's north coast.

The French in Morocco

French rule over Morocco followed a unique path. Although the French had been in neighboring Algeria since 1830, they were kept out of Morocco until 1912. The French came to control Morocco through a simple financial move. Morocco was deeply in debt. The French took over management of Morocco's finances and assumed control of the country too. Morocco was thought of as "independent" because the sultan consented to the protectorate when he signed the Treaty of Fez. But Morocco was not independent of France at all. The country was ruled by a colonial administrator.

The Moroccans were fortunate that the first administrator was General Louis Lyautey (right). He is said to have virtually created the modern nation of Morocco. He later was given the title of "Marshall" and this is how he is generally known. Marshall Lyautey, who spoke Arabic, truly admired the people he ruled. He approached Morocco as a society with an ancient and honorable history. It once had a thriving economy and a class of cultured and well-educated people. He was determined to help the Moroccans regain their past glory and devoted himself to one of his great loves—building cities. When Lyautey took over in 1912, Morocco had no bridges or railways and had only the most miserable roads,

hospitals, and schools. There were no maps of the country and there was no rule of law.

Lyautey was in charge until 1925. He was particularly careful not to construct new, French buildings within the ancient Arab sections. He was respectful of the customs of the Moroccan people and is considered to have preserved the ancient cities of Morocco that were so important to the nation's cultural heritage.

The port city of Tangier had been declared an international zone by 1912 and was administered by a group of European nations. These divisions continued through the period of the French protectorate, from 1912 to 1956.

French Settlement

In order to fill the many jobs that were needed to create this modern society, the French called upon their own people. Instead of training the Moroccans, they encouraged French people to settle in Morocco. French farmers were promised inexpensive land where they could plant vineyards, citrus groves, and orchards. The nation's agriculture, the heart of its economy at that time, was to be in the hands of these French settlers, known as *colons*, a French word that means "colonist" and "planter." More than anything else, this action divided Morocco into two parts, one for French-speaking people, the other for Arabs and Berbers. By planting the French people throughout the countryside, France created a strong claim to the territory. Eventually, the French army would be called in to protect French interests in Morocco.

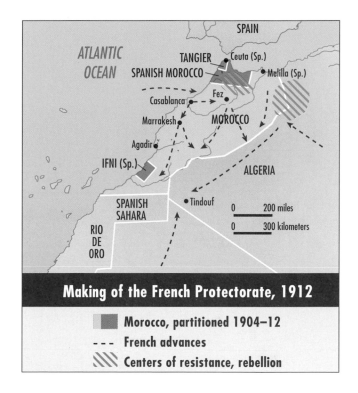

Making of the French Protectorate, 1912

- ▨ Morocco, partitioned 1904–12
- --- French advances
- ▨ Centers of resistance, rebellion

Berber Resistance

In spite of his achievements, Marshall Lyautey and his administration were bitterly resisted by the Berbers. They continued to fight for twenty years, holding out in the hills of the Rif and Atlas Mountains. Each of these tribes (for that is what they were called) was independent, and they often fought one

Abd al Krim led a revolt against the French.

another. They were particularly out of control in the region of the Rif Mountains that was part of the Spanish protectorate. Their leader, Abd al Krim, was a very effective military leader. He brought the warring tribes of the Rif Mountains together in 1924 and created a real government. He tried to gain independence from Spain, and from Morocco.

French Foreign Legion

Abd al Krim ruled over rebels who were so determined that it took a full-scale invasion by the French and Spanish to finally defeat them. More than 400,000 French and Spanish troops, along with the most modern military equipment of the day,

Troops led by Abd al Krim fighting the better-equipped French near Taza

were needed to bring peace to the region. Among them were the units known as the French Foreign Legion, a part of the French army made up entirely of soldiers from other countries. The Legionnaires of France fought bravely, but they were up against a very different kind of war. It took two years before they were able to bring the Rif rebellion under control.

Moroccan Unrest

By 1934, all of Morocco was under the control of one governing agency for the first time in its history. Unfortunately, the colonial administrators who followed Marshall Lyautey did not share his respect for the people,

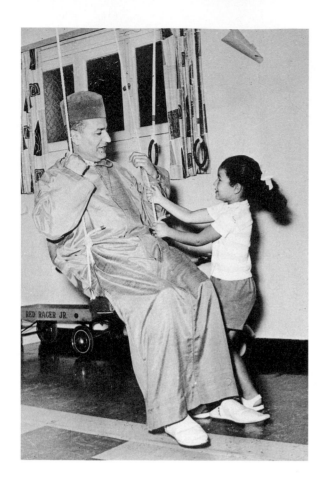

Sultan Ben Youssef, Mohammed V, relaxes with his daughter.

Sultan Ben Youssef on horseback

their customs, and their culture. Just when the Moroccans were ready to run their own affairs, the colonial office moved the country backward. They replaced the Moroccans in the civil service with French settlers. There was now a wave of revolt against colonial rule, both in Africa and around the world. The Moroccans wanted independence and their leader, Sultan Sidi Mohammed Ben Youssef, also known as Mohammed V, encouraged this movement.

Ben Youssef was a member of a Fez dynasty that was descended from Sherif, a brother of the prophet Muhammad. In 1927, at the age of eighteen, he was chosen by the French administration to be sultan. But Ben Youssef was proud to be a Moroccan and was sympathetic to the growing independence movement. He was both a modern and a traditional man. He had two wives, which is permitted under the religion of Islam.

World War II (1939–1945) hit like an earthquake in the colonies and protectorates controlled by European powers. Algeria, next to Morocco, was the site of one of the biggest battles of the war. While no major battles were fought in Morocco, the country was deeply involved in the war. France, which ran Morocco, was itself overrun by the German army in 1940, in the early days of the war. The country of France was occupied by the Germans.

When France fell to the Germans, the Moroccans saw a path to their own independence. If the French were unable to

Operation Torch

In 1942, the United States Army, under the direct command of General George Patton, landed 35,000 troops at three ports in Morocco. This was one phase of the entire North African campaign, called "Operation Torch." In two days, the French army in Morocco was overwhelmed by the Americans, and Morocco was liberated from German control. The United States established bases in Morocco to supply its soldiers fighting in Algeria and Europe. The United States would never have been able to stage the great battles of World War II without a base that was close to the action. Sultan Mohammed V enthusiastically supported the Allies' efforts to free France and Italy from the control of the Germans. Three hundred thousand Moroccans fought in World War II battles in southern Europe.

rule themselves, how could they insist on ruling Morocco? Sultan Mohammed V refused to support the government of Morocco, which was run by the French under the direction of the Germans. He showed great personal courage in refusing to carry out the orders given by the Germans. He personally protected the Jews living in Morocco.

Roosevelt in Casablanca

In 1943, U.S. President Franklin Delano Roosevelt came to Casablanca to meet with Britain's Prime Minister Winston Churchill and make plans to fight the Germans. This meeting

Sultan Mohammed V, U.S. President Franklin Delano Roosevelt, and British Prime Minister Winston Churchill (seated, left to right) met in 1943.

was a complete secret and was not known to the people in the United States until after President Roosevelt returned to Washington. During this crucial meeting, the two leaders agreed that the only acceptable end to the war was the complete surrender of the Germans and their allies, known as the Axis powers.

During his time in Casablanca, President Roosevelt met privately with Sultan Mohammed V, a meeting that has been described as the first time that the sultan "had ever been permitted to see a foreign dignitary alone, without French advisers standing by." This meeting, as well as Moroccan participation in the war against Germany, led the people to believe that France would grant their independence quickly. The sultan expected to have the support of the Americans. Unfortunately, neither Roosevelt nor Churchill was still in power in 1945 when the war ended. Whatever promises of support they had given toward Morocco's independence faded as the French returned to power.

Steps to Independence

The Istiqlal political party was formed and held its first meeting in Rabat in January 1944. *Istiqlal* means "independence." The party demanded full independence for Morocco and reunification of the parts that were under the control of France and Spain. It also demanded a democratic constitution that would give people a voice in the running of their country. Sultan Mohammed V approved this manifesto, but the French administrator refused to make any changes. The administrator was backed by the many French colonials who had settled in Morocco. They enjoyed their life and had no interest in seeing the Moroccans in charge. Nor did they want to return to France, which was still suffering from the terrible effects of the war.

When the sultan made a speech in Tangier in 1947 calling for independence for Morocco, the French responded by appointing General Alphonse Juin as resident general. He would not hear of any plans leading to independence. The French were determined to hold onto Morocco and General Juin was considered the right man for the job.

General Alphonse Juin

Sultan in Exile

Juin's hard line toward Sultan Mohammed Ben Youssef ultimately led to riots in Casablanca in December 1952 in which about 400 people were killed. The Istiqlal was outlawed by the French. By this time it had more than 80,000 active members as well as the support of several hundred thousand other Moroccans who believed in the drive for independence. The French saw that they would not be able to convince Ben Youssef to stop supporting the independence movement. They removed him from his leadership role and sent him into exile on August 20, 1953. He was first sent to the French island of Corsica, in the Mediterranean, but the French feared he was too close to Morocco and would be able to stir up trouble there. Later that year they sent him, with his family, to Madagascar.

The sultan's exile, and his continued fight for independence, made him more popular with the people. Even though he was not in Morocco, the sultan was the symbol of the independence the people wanted.

French Choose New Sultan

On that same day in August 1953, the French replaced Ben Youssef with another sultan, one who would do as they wished. He was Sidi Mohammed Ben Moulay Arafa. He did not press for Morocco's independence. The United States, which was strongly opposed to the removal of Ben Youssef, kept silent on this issue. It decided that its own political interests were more important. The United States wanted to be sure that U.S. air bases would be allowed to remain. They guaranteed an American military presence close to its cold-war enemy, the Soviet Union.

Fight for Independence

Even without the official Istiqlal political party, the people continued to press for independence. People began arming themselves to fight the French troops. Hundreds of people were killed. Even the Berbers joined in against the French. Finally the French government decided the only way to bring peace was to bring Sultan Mohammed Ben Youssef back to Morocco.

The sultan agreed to a constitutional monarchy, which would bring a measure of democracy to the country, something new for Morocco. Further steps were taken in 1955 that returned control of different aspects of the country to Morocco.

Sultan Mohammed V returns to Morocco.

On March 2, 1956, Morocco became an independent nation led by Sultan Mohammed Ben Youssef. With his return to power, the people had a leader who was also the religious head of the country.

When he became the leader of an independent Morocco, Mohammed V took the title of king, which he felt was more in keeping with the modern world. He wanted to create a new form of government—a constitutional monarchy. The people were promised a written constitution, a document that would tell them exactly what rights and privileges they had as Moroccan citizens.

In spite of his success at leading Morocco to independence, King Mohammed V now faced the task of creating a modern nation. The freedom enjoyed by Morocco soon unleashed a storm of political parties. Each one was anxious to promote its own cause and its own group. The rural people had quite different interests from the city people. These differences tended to coincide with the split between the Arabs and the Berbers—the Arabs were more influential in the cities, while the Berbers were more important in the farming areas. Younger Moroccans wanted to break with the whole idea of a royal leadership. Others wanted to increase the influence of Islam over the government. The king moved to secure his position by appointing his son Crown Prince Mulay Hassan as chief of staff of the new Royal Armed Forces.

With so many groups all trying to gain control, the king found it difficult to form a cooperative government. In 1960, King Mohammed V took direct leadership of the country, naming his son Hassan as his deputy. By 1961, the promised constitution was enacted. Morocco became a member of the Arab League, a group of countries whose national origins were Arabic.

Moroccan women members of the Istiqlal political party in 1955

Death of Mohammed V

In February 1961, King Mohammed V died suddenly following surgery. He had governed barely five years. The country was left in the hands of his son, 31-year-old Hassan II. He wasted no time in taking personal control of the government, naming himself prime minister and choosing a new cabinet of ministers. He also wrote a new constitution, which was put to a vote in December 1962. This constitution was accepted overwhelmingly. It established a two-house parliament.

State of Emergency

Political unrest exploded in 1965, largely stemming from a new order that all students over the age of seventeen had to go through a course of technical training. The students believed this was a plan to limit their access to the universities, and they began to protest. Peaceful demonstrations quickly turned violent when unemployed workers joined them. The police and the army eventually regained order but only at a cost of some 400 lives. Unable to gain political control of the country, Hassan II declared a state of emergency in 1965, putting off elections until after a new constitution could be written.

Morocco's role as an Arab nation was put to the test during the June 1967 war between Egypt and Israel. When Israel defeated the Arab forces in six days, the Jews of Morocco were threatened. Although the Moroccan government tried to reassure the Jewish population, about 80,000 Jews left the country over the next few years. Political turmoil continued through the end of the 1960s, and in July 1970, King Hassan announced yet another constitution. This one gave the king even more power than he had before. Like the other votes, it was passed almost unanimously, by 98.7 percent of the voters.

Although the state of emergency was declared over in 1970, unrest continued. Economic problems, administrative problems, and especially a lack of opportunity for genuine participation in the government created a continual sense of frustration among large parts of the population.

Attempt to Overthrow the King

On July 10, 1971, as guests were celebrating Hassan II's birthday, a group of young army officers staged an attack on the king, his guests, and his staff and attempted to gain control of the government. Whenever a group tries to overthrow the government in a country in Africa, it tries to take control of the radio. That is how most people get their news. In this case, the army did take control of the radio and immediately broadcast the news that the king was dead. But the regular forces quickly gained control, and the king's appearance proved that the "news" was not true.

Although the revolt was over in a day, the attempt to take over the government told the king quite clearly that change was needed. A new constitution in 1972 was followed by another attack on the king, when his airplane was fired on by Moroccan Air Force jets. In response, Hassan II assumed even more control of the country, and the armed forces in particular.

The king needed to make a grand gesture that would unite the people in a common goal. He found the perfect subject: the land to the south of Morocco that was known as the Spanish Sahara. Outside Morocco, it is known as the Western Sahara.

The Western Sahara

The question of who governs the territory formerly known as the Spanish Sahara is still in dispute, but not in Morocco. There, support for the king's moves to reclaim the territory is absolute. This is the issue that Hassan II used to unite the Moroccan people.

This Sahara region was colonized by Spain in 1884. The small population was nomadic, moving frequently with their herds of sheep and goats, traveling by camel. They were always in search of water and grazing land. In the 1930s, the Spanish established the town of Laayoune and made it their headquarters. It remains the economic center of the region. Until 1963, Spanish Sahara had very little to offer in the way of resources other than spectacular sand dunes. As the wind blows over the dunes, it ripples the sands into ridges that are constantly on the move. The dunes seem to march, very slowly, across the landscape. Footprints never linger on the dunes; the wind blows them away.

Then, in 1963, phosphates were discovered at Boukra, sixty miles inland. Phosphates, which are used as fertilizers, play a vital role in agriculture. The region suddenly looked like a place worth fighting for. The people of the territory, called Sahrawis, did not think of themselves as belonging to

The Green March to claim
the Spanish Sahara in 1975

any country. They crossed the "borders"—invisible lines in the sand—whenever they needed to. A group was formed that claimed to represent them. This group, the Polisario, is based in neighboring Algeria. Spain turned to the United Nations for help in resolving the conflict. The United Nations reported that most of the Sahrawis wanted to be independent and should be given a chance to vote.

The Green March

The vote, called a referendum, never took place. King Hassan II decided to reclaim the territory for Morocco in 1975. He felt he was reclaiming it because it had been part of Morocco in the eleventh century. In a dramatic step, he summoned the people of Morocco to march across the border into Spanish Sahara. He called this the Green March because green is the holy color of Islam.

In 1975, 350,000 unarmed civilians went on the Green March, starting from the southern Morocco town of Tarfaya. The march was a very powerful symbol of Morocco's determination to hold on to the territory. An agreement was reached in which the region was divided between Morocco, which got two-thirds, and Mauritania, which got the southern third.

Moroccan soldiers guard a fortification near Laayoune.

The Polisario continued to wage an armed war against troops of Morocco and Mauritania. At the same time, they gathered the Sahrawi people into refugee camps in Algeria. Unwilling to continue fighting, Mauritania gave up its third in 1979. Morocco took control of the entire territory, which it still occupies. This region increases Morocco's size by nearly half. Morocco has divided the region into four provinces, in addition to the country's thirty-six other provinces.

The Sand Wall

In 1980, Morocco began the amazing task of building a wall of sand across the entire territory. This wall was a military installation, created by soldiers with bulldozers. Over a period of four years, sections of the wall were built until it stretched all the way from Algeria to the Atlantic Ocean. This protected an area the Moroccans refer to as the "useful Sahara." At the height of the war, it was guarded by 100,000 Moroccan soldiers.

Will There Be a Referendum?

Year after year, the issue of the Western Sahara was supposed to be decided by a referendum, but the vote was constantly postponed. There was always something to argue about, especially how to decide who was eligible to vote. Year after year, deadlines passed. Meanwhile the Moroccan government was pouring money into the territory. Where there had been nothing but a rough track, they built a road all the way to the Mauritania border. They turned the tiny desert town of Laayoune into a city of about 200,000.

By the beginning of 1999, when the registration of voters in the region had reached 147,000, there was still considerable doubt about whether the referendum would ever be held. The United Nations, which secured a cease-fire in the war between the Polisario and the Moroccan army, was questioning whether the entire operation was workable. Moroccans of every walk of life have no such doubts. They say, "Why should there be a referendum? It's part of Morocco, and it will always be part of Morocco."

Modern Morocco

A constitutional monarchy is a form of government that stands on two very different legs. Although the country has a constitution and the citizens elect members of the parliament, the leader of the country is not elected. The monarch, the king, inherits his position from his father. In this way, Morocco combines its ancient heritage with a modern form of government.

64

Morocco has been working to improve its constitution and create a more democratic government, but much of the power is in the hands of the king. A prime minister, who is the head of the administration, is named by the king. The number of provinces has grown to forty in an effort to create a closer connection between the government and the people. The head of each province is the king's representative and is chosen by the king.

King Hassan II at the opening of Parliament

Elected Government

The House of Representatives, the country's legislature, has 306 seats. The people vote directly for 206 of these seats, representing about two-thirds of the total. The other one-third—100 seats—are reserved for trade unions and professional groups. All men and women who are twenty years old are eligible to vote.

In addition to the four constitutions written between 1961 and 1992, significant amendments to the constitution were enacted in 1996. A one-house legislature was replaced with a two-house legislature. In the 1997 legislative elections, the king gained even more control of the government. He has the power to dismiss the entire 306-member legislature.

In a Muslim country, the law is spelled out in the Koran (or Qur'an) and the king, as the nation's spiritual leader, is

Opposite: **A mounted palace guard, Rabat**

NATIONAL GOVERNMENT OF MOROCCO

The King

> REGENCY COUNCIL

> COUNCIL OF MINISTERS
> ▼
> PRIME MINISTER
> ▼
> MINISTERS OF STATE (2)
> ▼
> MINISTRIES (12)

> SUPREME COUNCIL FOR NATIONAL
> DEVELOPMENT AND PLANNING

> SUPREME COUNCIL FOR EDUCATION

Parliament

> HOUSE OF REPRESENTATIVES
> (306 SEATS)

> HOUSE OF COUNSELLORS

Judiciary

> SUPREME COUNCIL OF THE JUDICIARY
> ▼
> SUPREME COURT
> ▼
> COURTS OF APPEALS (15)
> ▼
> REGIONAL AND LOCAL TRIBUNALS

Pages of a 16th-century Koran

also the law. But in practice, in Morocco, the religious law, called *sharia*, is used only in cases that have to do with the individual's role as a Muslim. In other matters, the courts follow laws that follow the French example. The proceedings, however, are conducted in Arabic.

The King

King Hassan II has ruled Morocco since his father, Mohammed V, died in 1961. He was thirty-one years old when he took over and is the only leader most of the people know.

Morocco had been ruled by a sultan since the seventeenth century, the beginning of the Alawite dynasty. Mohammed V was sultan during the last years of the French colonial period. As part of the Alawite dynasty, Mohammed V's family traces its ancestry all the way back to the prophet Muhammad.

King Hassan II receives respects from a military officer. The king's sons stand behind him.

King Hassan II is the nation's spiritual leader as well as its political leader. Under his rule, there have been efforts to bring more democratic rule to the nation. Hassan II will be succeeded by his son, Crown Prince Sidi Moulay Hassan.

Hassan II doesn't look the way we might expect a king to look. He doesn't dress in royal robes or wear a crown. But he has enormous power, far more than Queen Elizabeth II of Britain, whose role is more symbolic. Hassan II is known to have two wives and several daughters, in addition to the crown prince and another son.

Flag of Morocco

As far back as the seventeenth century, when Morocco was ruled by the Alawites, the country has had a red flag. In 1915, a green, five-pointed star was added to the center of the flag. This star is known as the Seal of Suleyman. Green is the color of Islam because it is the color of life in the desert. The symbol of that life is Allah, who is seen as an oasis in the desert. This has been the country's flag since 1915.

Rabat: Did You Know This?

Morocco's capital city of Rabat began as a fortified monastery, called a *ribat* in Arabic, in the tenth century. It is one of Morocco's four imperial cities, all of which have been the capital at some point in history. (The other three are Marrakesh, Meknès, and Fez.) Through the centuries, Rabat grew and prospered, only to be abandoned when a new dynasty took power. When Rabat was the Almohad capital during the twelfth century, the splendid gates that guard the old city were built. Then, the Almohads lost power and Fez became the new capital. Rabat came back to life in 1627, this time as the center of a ring of pirates. They raided foreign boats that came into the Mediterranean and the Atlantic. They were so powerful that they forced foreign powers to negotiate with them.

In 1786, when the United States was just ten years old, George Washington signed a treaty of friendship with Sidi Mohammed Ben Abdullah. In 1912, the first resident-general of the French protectorate made Rabat his administrative center. He planned a modern European city but left the old city as it was. The sultan decided to live in Rabat too and built a new palace there. When Morocco became independent in 1956, Rabat was ready to take its place as the new country's capital. It combines the best of the old and the new. The whole history of Rabat is told in the walls and buildings that still stand in the medina—the old section.

Rabat's population is 1,472,000 (1990 estimate, greater city). In January, the average daily temperature is 60°F (16°C). In July, the average daily temperature is 72°F (22°C).

Minerals, Migrants, and Tourists

In spite of its climate and its many mountain ranges, Morocco is still an agricultural country. Half of all the people working in the country work on the land. Many of them raise just enough food for their own use, while others are employed on huge farms that produce food for export to Europe.

IN A GOOD YEAR, WHEN THERE IS ENOUGH RAIN, Morocco can raise two-thirds of the food needed to feed its own people. This is the best record in the region. But Morocco makes most of its money from just one resource—phosphate.

A Berber woman harvesting barley by hand

Mining

The principal mineral in Morocco is phosphate. Phosphates are used as fertilizers, a vital part of agriculture. Phosphate mining only began in 1921. Morocco has about two-thirds of the world's phosphate reserves. Exporting phosphates and the products made from phosphates brings in about one-fourth of Morocco's export income. One-third of the country's manufacturing is also related to phosphates. However, the United States and the former Soviet Union produce more phosphates than Morocco. In 1997, Morocco produced more than 21 million metric tons of phosphates, which earned U.S.$1.5 billion for the economy.

Although there are phosphate mines in Morocco itself, the best-quality phosphate is found in the Western Sahara. After the ore is mined, it must be transported to a port for shipment out of the country. At a mine called Boukra a conveyor belt was built that measures almost 60 miles (96.5 km) long. It stretches right across the country, all the way to the coast near Laayoune.

Opposite: **Harvesting dates**

A phosphate plant near
Morocco's west coast

Fruits and Vegetables

Morocco has learned to make the most of its resources,
especially water. For any country on the edge of the desert, the
water supply is a constant concern and for that reason water is
treasured. It is a surprise to discover that Morocco has become

a successful producer of fruits and
vegetables. It relies on a modern
system of irrigation and plants its
crops in greenhouses, where the
climate can be controlled. Oranges
are its most important crop but it is
well known for its tangerines and
lemons. Fresh vegetables are a popular part of the Moroccan diet, and
the local markets always have a
wide variety. Morocco has become
a major supplier of fruits and
vegetables to Europe as well.

Agricultural production
on the Atlantic coast

Palm Trees

Date palm trees are a common sight in Morocco wherever there is water. Growing at an oasis or alongside the pool in a hotel, the trees represent the country itself. They grow straight up, without branches, and their trunks don't get wider with age. Instead, the trees get taller and their leaves, known as palms, grow out of the top of the trees. Palm trees can grow to be 100 feet (30 m) in height. The dates are very sweet berries. The date picker must climb the tree to harvest the dates. Palm trees are grown in plantations that now cover 200,000 acres (80,940 ha). A total of 4.7 million palm trees are being grown in Morocco, and every part of the tree is used. The trunks are used in building; the leaves are woven into mats or other household goods. Sections of leaves, called fronds, are used as fencing and as wind blockers.

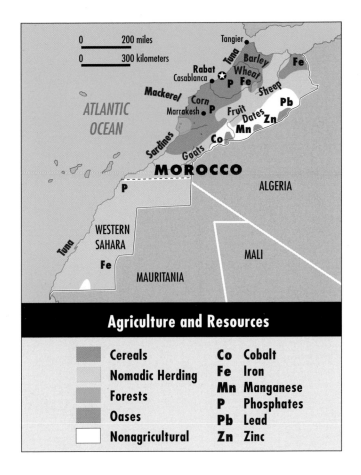

Fishing

Fishing, especially for sardines, is a major industry in Morocco. In addition to the fishing itself, many people are employed in canning and packing the catch. All together, 100,000 people have jobs in this area. The major fishing

Fishers in Agadir

port is Agadir, known as the biggest sardine-fishing port in the world. Fish auctions are held at Agadir every afternoon when the boats come back in with their catch of sardines as well as sea perch, mullet, and tuna. They also harvest shrimp, lobster, and crayfish from these waters. With all this fresh fish, it's not surprising that Agadir's restaurants are known for their wonderful fish dishes.

What Morocco Grows, Makes, and Mines

Agriculture (1997)

Beet sugar	2,595,000 metric tons
Wheat	2,316,000 metric tons
Barley	1,324,000 metric tons

Manufacturing (1994) *(in Moroccan dirhams)*

Food	10,159,000,000
Chemical products	5,951,000,000
Textiles	4,108,000,000

Mining (1994) *(in Moroccan dirhams)*

Phosphate rock	3,600,000,000
Zinc	277,000,000
Lead	234,000,000

Manufacturing

Morocco's people are very skillful craftspeople, and their skills are being used more and more in other industries. Assembling and sewing clothing has become an important industry, along with metalworking. Sewing is not a home industry. The people come to work in large plants built by foreign firms. The finished products are exported to Europe. Morocco supplies the labor, while Europe supplies both the technical knowledge and the market. Unfortunately, Morocco has a long way to go to create enough jobs for its own people.

Exporting Workers

The most significant fact about Morocco's economy is a matter of simple arithmetic: Each year the number of people who come into the workforce is greater than the number of jobs available. The birthrate has declined in recent years, but the population is still very young. An estimated 70 percent of

The large number of young people in Morocco contributes to high unemployment.

the people in Morocco are under 25 years old.

Although the country needs new jobs, the government was forced to reduce the number of its employees. This was done to lower the country's budget deficit. The result was a huge increase in the number of unemployed people, especially young people who haven't been able to get into the job market. At the same

Signs in Arabic and French. French is a reminder of Morocco's colonial past.

time, people continue to leave the rural areas, drawn to the excitement of the cities. That creates even more unemployment.

Workers have been leaving Morocco for years to find work. This is not a question of going to another town or another part of the country, but of leaving the country. The closest place to find employment is in Europe, across the Mediterranean Sea. Most workers go to France, the former colonial ruler of Morocco, where they can speak the local language.

The number who leave, estimated at about 1.8 million people, represents 20 percent of the country's working-age population. The people with the least chance of finding a job are high school graduates. About one-third of them are unemployed. University graduates, a far smaller group, have an unemployment rate of about 11 percent. Professionals go as far away as Belgium to find work, because it too is a French-speaking country.

At one time, Europe welcomed these migrant workers. The Moroccans were willing to do the kinds of jobs the Europeans would not do themselves. Now, however, many other migrants are competing for the same jobs. In addition, some European economies have become weaker and need the jobs for their own people. Tensions have increased, and there have been clashes because of the cultural differences between the French, who are mostly Christians, and the Moroccans, who are Muslims.

Morocco is trying to strengthen its relationship with Europe, but on a more equal basis. Morocco tried to join the European Union (EU), a group of countries that will have the same currency and that have broken down the borders that separate them. Although Morocco was refused membership in the EU, it has been given special access to the markets of Europe. Some of its products may be sold there without import taxes. Morocco sees itself as an extension of Europe, not as a part of the African economy. Indeed, Morocco's number-one trading partner is France.

Tourism

Tourists have always found Morocco the perfect combination of the exotic and the familiar. World-class hotels and excellent food as well as good roads and transportation make traveling there comfortable. From these familiar bases, visitors can journey into the past by entering the *medinas*—the old walled cities—which are a patchwork quilt of sounds, smells, sights, and textures. Tiny shops, often lit only by a single bulb, are

Djemaa el Fna

In Marrakesh, there is a place so fantastic it seems to be a set for a movie about a mythical city. But *Djemaa el Fna* is no myth. The name means "square of death," and executions were once held there. This large square in the heart of the city is an open-air entertainment that doesn't require a ticket. Moroccans simply arrive and begin performing for the constant stream of visitors. The local residents come to visit the shops that border the square, but they stay to watch the snake charmers, the dancers and musicians, the storytellers and the water sellers.

Women weaving a rug, which may be sold to tourists

open to passersby. Crafts for sale are jammed into every available space while at the same time, craftsmen work on new pieces. Sons learn from their fathers, as they have done through the centuries. The techniques, and the patterns, are repeated over and over again.

A tourist in Morocco is able to walk through the pages of history by visiting the imperial cities and the ruins at Volubilis. Every part of Morocco is a contrast between ancient and modern. Among the sights on every tourist's list are the imperial cities, as well as Tangier and Casablanca. In Fez, tourists visit the Kairouyine University. In Marrakesh, everyone wants to see the Koutoubia Mosque, named for the booksellers who gathered in front of it in the twelfth and thirteenth centuries. This city, which began life as an oasis for the Almoravids in the eleventh century, is today one of the most compelling places for visitors and citizens alike. The walled city is entered through one of its massive gates, each one a beautiful archway of stone.

Tourism brings more than 2 million people to Morocco each year, more than half of them from Europe. These tourists contribute enormously to the economy and are the most visible employer in Morocco. Hundreds of thousands of people work directly in tourism and indirectly through the crafts and construction industries. Tourists buy crafts, stay in hotels, and employ local guides. They create a need for hotel construction, for education, and for road-building.

The Medina

Every old city in Morocco has a medina, but none can compare to the one in Fez (left and below). It has been described as a maze, a puzzle, a place that even mapmakers can't cope with. It is all of that, and more. Here, where Moroccans come to shop and tourists come to look, the streets are merely passageways, sometimes so narrow you can easily touch both walls of the buildings as you walk by. People share those narrow passages with donkeys loaded with all sorts of goods. The donkeys have the right of way—and to make room for them to pass, you often have to jump into any doorway you find. In the heart of the medina of Fez is the tannery. The smells from the animal skins and the dyes burn the eyes and insult the nose, but the products that emerge are beautiful.

To the people who live in the medina, it's all quite simple. They have their own neighborhoods and they know every inch of these alleys. Even in the middle of the crowded medina, the inside of a home is a private place. The medinas were built within high walls for protection against invaders.

The medinas of Fez and Marrakesh have been named World Heritage sites. This designation honors the great architecture of the medinas, especially the walls, the monumental entrance gates, and the ancient mosques.

Just as important, tourists bring a sense of the outside world directly to the heart of Morocco. They show the people a different way of living, another way for men and women to be together.

Bargaining

It is nearly impossible to buy anything in Morocco without bargaining. Set prices and price tags are not available in the markets, where all the interesting crafts are found. The first rule of thumb about bargaining is simple: Never accept the first price the merchant quotes. It's the beginning of a game, and it's a game the Moroccans never tire of playing.

High Up in Morocco

While most visitors come to enjoy the ancient sites and beautiful beaches, a very determined group comes to challenge Morocco's mountains. Jebel Toubkal, the highest mountain, offers the biggest challenge, but even the smaller ones are very difficult because they are so sharp and rugged. Climbers take about a week to climb Jebel Toubkal, staying overnight along the way so they can get used to the high altitude.

It's wise for climbers to hire a Berber guide to take them up Jebel Toubkal. Even experienced climbers who are not familiar with the mountain can get lost. In a region where the weather can change virtually in a minute, and where snow can fall at the most unlikely time of year, getting lost can be dangerous. The guide is also an introduction to the culture of the Berbers. The guide cooks the evening meal of tajine or couscous and brews the tea. It's a very special way to experience the beauty and majesty of Morocco.

Lights, Camera, Morocco!

A poster advertising the movie *Casablanca*

Morocco has been used as a film set for 100 years but the most famous movie about Morocco, *Casablanca*, was made in Hollywood! That's because it was made while World War II was still taking place. The movie shows how Morocco was a safe haven for people fleeing Europe during the war. These people would do anything to get "transit visas," documents that would allow them to travel on to Lisbon, Portugal. From there, they could get to North America, and safety. Even though the movie was made on a set, it captures the sense of danger and despair of that time. It also shows the strange relationship between the French Moroccans and the Germans who governed them during the war.

Filmmakers love Morocco because the light is so beautiful and because the ancient buildings can stand in for many cultures throughout history. The Sahara can be the desert in a half-dozen North African countries. Even Shakespeare's *Othello* was filmed here, on the twelfth-century walls of Essaouira. The first film ever made in Morocco was a French short called *The Moroccan Horseman*. It was made by the Lumière Brothers in 1897. Morocco was used in *Lawrence of Arabia*, for a shot that depicted the country of Jordan. In 1997, Martin Scorcese's film about the Dalai Lama and Tibet, *Kundun*, was shot almost entirely in Morocco.

Colorful Currency

The basic unit of Moroccan money is the dirham. Paper money is available ranging from 10 dirhams to 200 dirhams. There are also 1-dirham, 5-dirham, and 10-dirham coins. Other coins are worth one-tenth and one-twentieth of a dirham. The money features a portrait of King Hassan II on one side. On the opposite side are images including buildings, flowers, and musical instruments. In 1999, 9.50 Moroccan dirhams (DH) were equal to U.S.$1.

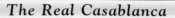

The Real Casablanca

Although Casablanca has its old sections, the city shows a very modern face, especially at the port. Modern glass-covered shopping centers selling luxury goods and filled with elegant restaurants provide a vivid contrast to the medina that rests in the very center of the city. The city has a lively, Western air about it. Casablanca's beachfront, known as the Boulevard de la Corniche, combines beaches and swimming pools with cafés, hotels, and restaurants. Here, local people stroll along the shore, enjoying the sea air or visiting the Sinbad Amusement Park. The modern town, planned by Marshall Lyautey, was built in the style of the medina, but with pleasant squares and neat streets that follow a pattern. Casablanca lives up to its name. It is a city of white houses.

Casablanca is Morocco's largest city.

CHAPTER

SEVEN

Vibrant Ancient Cultures

The first permanent culture of Morocco was that of the Berbers, who came to the area about 4,000 years ago. No one knows where the Berbers came from although there are many theories. Wherever it was— Europe or Asia are the usual guesses—they were the ancestors of most of Morocco's population today.

83

Berbers in the Atlas Mountains

A LMOST HALF OF TODAY'S POPULATION IS BERBER, tied to the Berber culture and speaking Berber as their first language. The most isolated Berbers, who live in remote parts of the Rif and the Atlas Mountains, speak only Berber, although tourists are making their way into some of the most remote areas and this is likely to change.

> ## The Berber Language

The Berber language was an oral language—it was never written down. The culture, history, crafts, and everything else the Berbers knew were passed down from one person to another through speech. For thousands of years, until the coming of the Arabs in the seventh and eighth centuries A.D., Berber was the only language of Morocco. The name *Berber* comes from *Barbarus*, a name given to the people by the Romans, who considered them barbarians—uncivilized. But it is not the name the people call themselves. The great mountains of Morocco kept the various Berber groups apart, and their language developed into different dialects. These dialects are so different that one group cannot understand the others. There is no single word for Berber. In the High Atlas, some Berbers call themselves *imazighen*, which means "free people."

Previous page: **A young Berber of the Ait Haddidu tribe**

The Berber language might have developed into a written language if the Arabs and Islam had not arrived. The spread of Islam was tied to the Koran, the Muslim holy book that was written in Arabic. In order to read the Koran, you had to be able to read Arabic. The Arabic language itself had only begun to be written down a few centuries before. The beautiful Arabic script was developed especially to write down the words of the prophet Muhammad.

The use of Berber diminished as the use of Arabic spread. Berber has never been taught in schools. Berbers who want to deal with the rest of Morocco must learn Arabic or French or both. At least half of Morocco's Berbers also speak Arabic.

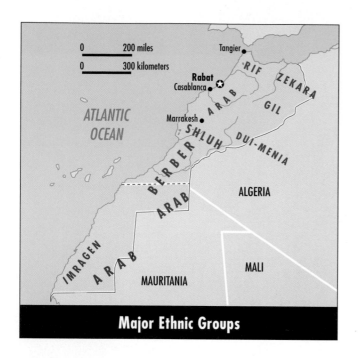

Major Ethnic Groups

Who Lives in Morocco?

Arab-Berber	99.1%
Other	0.7%
Jewish	0.2%

The Arabic Language

Arabic, the language of North Africa as well as some of the countries of the Middle East, was brought to Morocco in the seventh century by the Muslim converts from the Arabian Peninsula. However, the Arabs were not more than 10 percent of the Moroccan population. They mixed with Berber women from the beginning, creating a population in which nearly everyone has some Berber blood.

Their language dominated, however, because they moved throughout the region and were not restricted to the mountains. They claimed the cities, which have larger populations than the rural areas. In addition to being the language of the country's religion, Arabic has been the language of trade for at least 500 years. About three-quarters of all Moroccans speak Arabic.

In English, we have borrowed the Arabic word *bazaar* to mean a gathering of shops in one place. Many people know the word *kasbah*, also spelled *casbah*. Although the original kasbahs were forts, they have become known more as places of entertainment.

In 1965, a law was passed that made Arabic the only language that could be used for any legal proceeding, including deeds. Although all schoolchildren are taught in Arabic, French is offered as a second language when students reach high school. Before independence, the Arabic language was not permitted in schools.

French continues to play an important role in Morocco. Anyone dealing with Europeans finds French very useful, and the country's continued ties to France make it natural that French continue to be used. The king is fluent in French and often uses it in daily life.

The Arabic Alphabet

Arabic letters are written in a flowing script that uses 28 symbols for the letters, or sounds, of the alphabet. Its graceful forms came into widespread use as a decorative element in part because Islam does not permit the use of images that portray humans or animals.

A Young Country

The total population of Morocco is just over 30 million people. Only 4 percent of the people are older than sixty-five. About half the people in the country are under the age of twenty, and this has created an economic problem. The business and industries of Morocco cannot keep up with the number of people looking for work, especially those who graduate from high school but do not go on to universities. Although almost half the people still live in rural areas, Casablanca, Morocco's largest city, now has more than 3 million people, about 10 percent of the population. Many of them live in the sprawling slums that have grown up around the city as people flood in from the rural areas looking for work.

Children on their way home from school in Marrakesh

Women university students in Rabat

Education

At the time of independence, only 10 percent of Moroccan children were in primary school. At that time, when there were nearly 2 million Moroccan children in the territory, only 15,000 boys (no girls) were in high school and just 350 were in university. Literacy remains a challenge for Morocco. Although about 50 percent of the people can read and write, the percentage of men, who can read (61 percent) is almost double that of women who can read (32 percent). Literacy is much lower among older adults.

Men are nearly twice as likely to be able to read as women because more boys are sent to school. Morocco's high birthrate makes it impossible for the country to build enough schools and train enough teachers to keep up with the population growth.

Spain in Morocco

Spanish is the first language of a small number of Moroccans who live in the regions that are still controlled by Spain. In 1988, the northern cities of Ceuta and Melilla, on the Mediterranean coast, were formally annexed to Spain. Morocco agreed to this because Spain promised to help Morocco sell its produce in the European Union. But no treaty was needed to make the two cities completely Spanish. They have their own Spanish customs and immigration. Ceuta is an ancient city near the Strait of Gibraltar. It was a

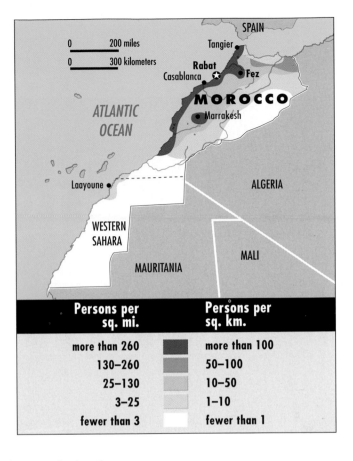

strategic port and was fought over by many powers before the Spanish won control in 1580. Ceuta's culture is Catholic, not Muslim.

Melilla is more of a mixture of Spanish and Moroccan cultures. It has no real economy other than the smuggling of goods, including kif and hashish, drugs derived from the hemp plant. This is a huge, illegal business in Morocco, amounting to U.S.$2 billion a year. The trade makes Melilla a threat to Morocco's relations with Europe and the European Union. Both Ceuta and Melilla are the remains of a coastal strip along the Mediterranean that was once controlled entirely by Spain.

Spain also once controlled Sidi Ifni, on the coast south of Agadir. This strip of land was acquired after Spain won a brief war with Morocco in 1860. Across from Sidi Ifni lie the Canary Islands, acquired by Spain in 1479. Although Sidi Ifni is now part of Morocco, it remains an important connection to the Canaries. Flights connect the two regions, and the waters between them are very important fishing grounds.

The northern Spanish towns in Morocco continue to have a strong connection to Spain. Migrant workers from this region travel to Spain, rather than France, because they speak the language. The old colonial ties still play a role in modern Morocco.

CHAPTER

EIGHT

Religious Harmony

Islam, the official religion of Morocco, is at the heart of daily life. It is part of the fabric of the country and can be felt by even the most casual visitor. The sound of the *muezzin* calling people to prayer is as regular as the sun rising. The right to religious freedom is guaranteed in the country's constitution. These two facts are not contradictions to Muslims, people who follow the Islamic religion.

LTHOUGH TOLERANCE OF OTHER RELIGIONS IS NOT
followed in many Muslim countries, it is one of the basic laws
of Islam. It is believed that the "People of the Book" (those who
follow the Bible) should be allowed to follow their own religion
as long as they recognize that the Muslim authorities rule the
nonreligious aspects of life. In practice this means that most
aspects of daily life are carried out under the laws of the religion
of Islam. Religion and government are not considered separate
structures in Morocco. In practical terms, this is not an issue in
Morocco, where nearly 99 percent of the people are Muslims.

**Religions
of Morocco**

Muslim	98.7%
Christian	1.1%
Jewish	0.2%

Opposite: **A muezzin calls
the faithful to prayer**

Jews and Christians in Morocco

There was a Jewish quarter in Marrakesh, known as the
mellah. So many trades were forbidden to Jews, they had
little to choose from except working as common laborers, or
as moneylenders if they had the resources.
Moneylending is against the law of Islam.
The Jews gained full status with Muslims
when the protectorate was declared in
1912. They came under the vigorous
protection of the sultan of Morocco, who
said they were "just as Moroccan as the
Muslims." But when Morocco became
independent, the Jews feared that they
would not do well under an Islamic

**A Jewish father and son in
Marrakesh in the 1950s**

government. They began to emigrate to the new Jewish state of Israel in large numbers after 1948. About 7,000 Jews still live in Morocco.

The number of Europeans who live in Morocco, mostly French and some Spanish, declined from 400,000 in 1958 to about 100,000 today. They make up most of the Christian population.

Religion and Daily Life

Islam, like most religions, is interpreted differently in the various regions where it is practiced. Some nations follow a very strict interpretation of the laws of Islam. The religious leaders, called *imams*, tell the people exactly how to live their lives. In

Muslims, who do not drink alcohol, in a soda bar

Moroccan women are free
to choose whether they
wear the veil.

Morocco, people are much freer to decide things for themselves. They are allowed to watch television, if they wish, or
listen to Western programs on the radio. In Morocco, women
are free to choose whether they will wear the veil, but in practice they are also influenced by their families. Unmarried
women more often do not wear the veil, while married women
often do. Some Berbers who don't wear the veil in their villages wear it when they come to the city to sell their crafts.
Whether they wear the veil or not, women in Morocco have
much more freedom than they do in more conservative Islamic
countries. Women play a role in business and on television.
However, women generally do not have as much freedom as
men do. Often, after a woman marries, her life is very carefully
controlled, not only by her husband, but also by his family.

What Is Islam?

The religion called Islam began in the year A.D. 610 when Muhammad, a merchant in the town of Mecca in Arabia, began preaching the message he said he received from God, or *Allah*. Mecca was already a holy city, but one in which idols were worshiped by heathens—people who were not Christians or Jews. Muhammad's ideas were not well received by the other merchants in Mecca, who charged fees to those who worshiped these idols.

Muhammad finally left Mecca for Medina with his followers in the year 622. This became the first year in the Islamic calendar. Muhammad became the leader of all of Arabia, both as a spiritual figure and because he defeated his opponents in battle. Islam spread rapidly and soon became closely identified with the Arab world. Allah's message was written down by others and became the *Koran*, the Muslim holy book. The Koran guides Muslims in every aspect of their daily life.

Muhammad is known as the prophet of Allah. He described five religious duties for Muslims. The first is to declare their faith by affirming, "There is no God but Allah, and Muhammad is His prophet." Second, they are required to show their faith by praying five times a day: at dawn, noon, afternoon, sunset, and when night falls. Muezzins (right) call the faithful to prayer. A Muslim may pray anywhere at all but must face the city of Mecca. Men and women are separated when they pray, and women usually pray at home. Muslim men are required to attend services at a mosque on Fridays, the Muslim Sabbath.

The third religious duty of Muslims is to give money to the poor, and the fourth is to observe the specific requirements of the holy month of Ramadan. The fifth requirement, to make a *hadj* (or *hajj*)—a special pilgrimage to Mecca—is the most difficult to observe. This is considered the most holy aspect of a Muslim's life. A person who has made the hadj is known as a *hadji* and will carry this title with him for the rest of his life. Women may make the hadj but few do. A family will work to save the money so that one person can make the hadj. It is a great honor and a great responsibility.

Ramadan

The holy month of Ramadan requires a great deal of discipline from Muslims. They are not allowed to eat or drink anything from sunrise to sunset each day for the entire month. They are not allowed to smoke either. Only those who are healthy are required to follow these restrictions. Because the Muslim calendar is based on the cycle of the moon, which is 28 days, the month of Ramadan takes place in different seasons from year to year. It is most difficult to observe during the hot summer months but it is always a test of people's willpower.

Each afternoon, as the sun lowers, people close their shops and rush home, waiting for the time when they are permitted to start the evening meal. Every evening is a little celebration and many people stay up very late, stretching out the sweet time when they are allowed to eat and drink. The month begins and ends with the sighting of the new moon, that slender crescent shape in the night sky. As the time approaches for the observances to end, people wait anxiously for word from the mosque that the end of Ramadan is declared. Although Ramadan is a difficult month, it is also a joyous one, for it celebrates the time when the sayings of Muhammad were gathered together in the Koran. The end of Ramadan is marked with the festival called Aid el-Fitr.

Medersa—Religious University

The first religious university, or *medersa*, was built in Fez. The Kairouyine Mosque and religious university in Fez began in 862 and was expanded in the tenth and twelfth centuries.

Students at a Koranic school
in the Kairouyine Mosque

Students lived at the universities, where they were taught not only the religion of Islam but also how to live according to the laws of Islam. One of the largest of these schools is Ali Ben Youssef Medersa in Marrakesh. It was built in the fourteenth century by Sultan Abou el Hassan and rebuilt in the mid-sixteenth century.

Before prayer can begin, each person must wash his or her hands and feet, so a fountain or washing area is always found in the central courtyard of the medersa and mosques. Muslims who do not have access to water, which occurs in many parts of the Islamic world, may use sand to clean themselves.

A man preparing to pray
washes his feet in a fountain
in the Kairouyine mosque.

The Mosque

The mosque is the center of religious life in Moroccan towns and cities. Entrance is usually restricted to Muslims. The mosque always indicates the direction of Mecca, so that the faithful can face in that direction. Jemaa, the Arabic word for mosque, simply means "assembly," a place where people come together. People are called to prayers by the muezzin, who stands outside the *minaret*, a square tower that rises up above the mosque. The sound of the muezzin can be heard over an entire neighborhood.

In preparation for praying, men line up in rows and kneel on the floor. They bow their heads down and touch the floor as a sign of respect. Prayers are said out loud, in unison. On Fridays, the imam delivers a sermon.

Until the 1990s, the largest mosque in Morocco was the Kairouyine Mosque in Fez. In 1980, King Hassan II directed that a great mosque be built. He wanted to create a mosque that would be located at the westernmost point of the entire Muslim world and so he chose Casablanca, on the Atlantic coast. Everything about this mosque (below), which opened in 1993, is on a huge scale. Twenty-five thousand men can gather in the main prayer hall at one time. A separate prayer hall was created on the upper level to hold 5,000 women hidden from the view of men.

A World of Contrasts

Traditions are not dusty old ideas that have no place in modern life. In Morocco, your culture is part of your family, and your family is part of your culture. The way people dress, the ceremonies they perform, the homes they live in, the relationship between men and women and their marriage rituals, are all part of the same cultural package and flow from the religion of Islam.

IF YOU WANT TO KNOW ABOUT MOROCCO, THE BEST PLACE to start is at home. The first thing you will learn is that the home is a very private place, meant only for the family and for very close friends.

Women eating together at home

The Home

The Muslim culture has played a major role in shaping the look of homes in Morocco. Because the lives of women and men are quite separate, even at home, houses are designed to help maintain that separation and to keep women out of

Opposite: **A folk festival in Marrakesh**

public view. The house itself is usually quite plain on the outside, giving no hint of the wealth or poverty of the people who live inside. There are no gardens or welcoming areas outside the house. There are no picture windows looking out onto the street, no balconies to watch the people passing by, and no way for people to look into the house. Private life and public life are quite separate in Morocco.

All the riches of the household are reserved for the people who live inside, and for those who visit them. The house is usually built around a courtyard that is open to the sky. This courtyard, usually with a tiled mosaic floor, often has a fountain in the center. Water is precious in Morocco and a fountain is the most generous gesture a family can make.

The family rooms are located around the courtyard, and there may be a second floor if the family is wealthy. It is usual for two generations to live together. When a couple marries, the bride goes to live in the groom's mother's house. Her life is controlled by her mother-in-law. The couple will have a bedroom in this house but the kitchen, the heart of the women's part of the house, is under the direction of the mother-in-law.

Marriage, Moroccan Style

If you come upon a wedding in Morocco, you may be invited to attend. Foreigners are considered to bring a marriage *baraka*—good luck. You should be prepared for a long stay. Traditional Moroccan weddings may last a week. There are separate parties for the men and for the women, for the bride's family and for the groom's family.

The bride is not seen much during the parties, a hint at the way she will live her life. The bride's friends and family help her make the bedding and carry it to her new home in the groom's house, in a great festive ceremony. The bride arrives, in a white, Western-style wedding gown, and then is taken to a private room in the groom's house. She doesn't come down for the party that night. The guests sit on cushions around the courtyard of the house and enjoy the music of live musicians.

An Arab bride dressed for the *selwa* ceremony

Henna

The use of henna for decoration is a tradition that is growing more popular, even with young modern women. In fact, henna has become quite fashionable now in the West and is even advertised along with lipstick and eyeliner. But the use of henna is an ancient tradition. The henna paste is made from the henna plant, smoked over a charcoal fire. It is applied to the hands and feet in lacy, geometric patterns that look like silk gloves. Once the pattern dries, it can last for a week or even a month, depending on how often the woman washes her hands or feet. Hands decorated with henna patterns represent the hand of Fatima, the prophet Muhammad's daughter.

Henna decoration is often created for special occasions. At the woman's party at a wedding, a professional henna artist may be hired to do all the women's hands. During the wedding celebrations, the bride is brought out of her room, and henna patterns are applied to her hands and feet. Women also have their hands done at the beginning of Ramadan.

There are male musicians for the men's party and female musicians for the women's party. Men and women dance at their own parties—men with men, and women with women. Men will be in the house during the women's party, but they sit in a separate room and watch the women dancing together from a short distance.

The bride is most visible when she is presented to the wedding guests during the *selwa* ceremony. The wedding garment and jewelry for an Arabic bride is so specific that it is rented for the occasion. The bride is dressed by women who bring the outfit with them. Then she is seated on a litter that is carried around the room by female attendants so she can be shown to the guests. After she has been seen by everyone, she is carried out of the room and is not seen again during this part of the celebration.

Moussems

Throughout the year, festivals called *moussems* are held to honor saints or teachers known as *marabouts*. These holy men developed at a time in Morocco's history when the people needed someone to help them understand the rapid changes taking place in their society. The moussems take place at the tombs of these holy men and are a mixture of religion, entertainment, and trade. They are held all over the country.

The moussem of Sidi Achmed ou Moussa is typical. Sheep and goats are slaughtered in the open while the market takes place down the hillside. Men may be seen praying all around the site. People travel long distances, often standing up in a truck, to get to the moussem. The biggest one of them all, attended by the king, is at Moulay Idriss. Some moussems are much more religious than others.

Fiancées Fair

Berber marriages, especially those in the high mountain regions, are quite different from Arabic marriages. The best-known place to see one is at Imilchil, in the High Atlas Mountains. This tiny village explodes with activity in September during the moussem known as the Fiancées Fair. The main purpose of the fair is the selling and trading of merchandise including camels, wool, and other basic needs. But it is also the place where Berbers come to find mates.

Men and women of the Ait Hadiddou Berber tribe make the difficult trip from their remote homes in the mountains on foot, by donkey, and sometimes by truck. The courtship is brief but it is also serious. The men and women know very little about each other, and the decision to marry carries enormous weight. These Berbers live in a very difficult area and in the harsh winter, a married couple have no one else to depend upon. They must work together as a team in order to produce enough food, clothing, and a house that will see them through to spring.

It's a kind of blind date, with a big difference. For those women who have been married before and are divorced, the men they meet at Imilchil will become their husbands within the three days of the moussem and market. A woman and a man will look at each other, making quick decisions. They

Berber men and women of the Ait Hadiddou tribe

concentrate on the eyes because they can't tell anything from the clothes—all the women dress alike in striped blue capes that are typical of their tribe. A woman who has been married before wears a pointed hood; a woman who has never married wears a rounded hood. They wear all their best silver and amber jewelry, some of it sewn onto a headband, to show that they have wealth and are important to their own families. Bold amber beads, the bigger the better, are worn over the cape. The men who are looking for brides wear white head-dresses. The man is looking for a strong woman, one who can do the farm work and bear children without any modern medical care. The woman wants to know how much land the man has and the work he does. Once the engagement is blessed at the tomb of Saint Mehreni, the couple may ride off together on the man's donkey.

Younger people who have never been married come to the fair to have their marriages blessed. This makes them officially engaged, although many may have been promised to each other for years before they reached the age of marriage. This is a more lighthearted time for them and a couple may stroll around for hours, barely allowing their fingers to touch. They are accompanied by relatives and friends who encourage them and keep an eye on the new couple.

A folk dancer wearing traditional jewelry

Berber Jewelry

A Berber woman without jewelry or with just one piece of jewelry is a very poor woman indeed. This is not merely a matter of wealth, but one of cultural identity. Some of these richly decorated pieces, called *fibulas*, play a role in fastening her garments, which do not have zippers or buttons. Berber jewelry follows the usual Islamic restrictions on design. The pieces are engraved with geometric patterns, or are made of coiled wires that form geometric shapes. Traditional jewelry usually includes dangling silver coins, many of them very old. Chains run from one piece to the other, and often several pieces are hooked together permanently. They must all be put on at the same time. Silver earrings don't go through the ear-lobe but are instead worn on chains that are sewn onto a headpiece. Green and yellow enamel as well as coral beads add color to the pieces.

This jewelry was traditionally made by Jewish metalsmiths who were prominent in the region until around 1950. As a result, much of the best old jewelry is disappearing from the market, and the new pieces often don't have the same rich decoration. There is also less interest in this traditional jewelry because it doesn't suit the Western clothes worn by modern Berber women.

Goulimine beads

Goulimine Beads

The southern city of Goulimine was a vital link in the caravan route to Timbuktu. One of the most beautiful commodities traded there are the Goulimine beads, known even today as "trading beads." These exquisite beads made of glass were called *millefiore* in Italy, where they were made. The word means "thousand flowers" because the beads look like a bunch of flowers in glass. They were so highly treasured by African chiefs that they were traded for Africans who became slaves. Huge baskets full of Goulimine

beads could be found for sale in the city. Now, the best beads are very rare, and very expensive.

Inspired by Morocco

Morocco has inspired many artists and writers who captured the sights, sounds, and moods of the people and the landscape. Perhaps the first known Moroccan writer was Ibn Battuta, sometimes called the Muslim Marco Polo. Ibn Battuta was a Berber who was born in Tangier in 1304. He traveled throughout the Muslim world and wrote about his impressions.

Mark Twain, author of *The Adventures of Tom Sawyer* and *The Adventures of Huckleberry Finn*, traveled through Morocco and based some of his work *Innocents Abroad* on his impressions. Paul Zweig captures his thoughts about Morocco and the desert in his autobiographical work *Three Journeys*. And

Fantasia

One of the most exciting moments at a moussem is the *fantasia*, a glorious example of Arab horsemanship. Turbaned men race their horses directly toward the spectators at top speed, shooting their rifles as they ride. Just as it seems they will crash into the people, they come to a complete stop. The dust clouds up around them and before anyone can take a breath, the horsemen are off to do it again.

Paul Bowles, an American who lived in Morocco for more than thirty years, brought the world to life in his books. In addition to foreigners writing about Morocco, the country has produced its own fine authors. Among the best known of these are Fatima Mernissi and Tahar Ben Jelloun.

Fatima Mernissi is best known for her study of women in Muslim societies. Her book *Beyond the Veil* was first published in 1973 and explains the forces pulling and pushing men and women in a rapidly changing world. She writes about polygamy, the practice of taking more than one wife at the same time, which is permitted in the Muslim religion. Tahar Ben Jelloun won the 1987 Prix Goncourt, a prestigious literary prize. Among his novels are *The Day of Silence at Tangier* and *The Sacred Night*.

Morocco (left) played against Brazil in the 1998 World Cup.

Soccer

For most people in Africa, there is only one sport to get excited about—soccer. Morocco is just as enthusiastic. It has one of the best teams in Africa and is a strong contender in all the events in which it takes part, including the Cup of Nations in Africa. At the 1998 World Cup in France, Mustapha Hadji was the star in the game against Norway. Although the game ended in a tie, the Moroccans in the audience were thrilled. The team went on to play Brazil, the best team in the world. They lost that game and did not move on to the next round.

World-Class Tennis

Morocco has a strong presence in the world of tennis, a fact that Pete Sampras knows very well. He came up against Moroccan Hicham Arazi in the Australian Open in 1998. Arazi, who was ranked forty-seventh in the world, played the number-one ranked player and gave him quite a fight. Sampras ultimately won but he was surprised by Arazi's speed and lightning serves. Although Arazi now lives in France, he plays on Morocco's Davis Cup team, which means he is considered among the best Moroccan players. Arazi also made it to the quarter-finals of the French Open in 1998. Another Moroccan player, Karim Alami, also did well at the Australian Open, winning his first two matches before losing to a French player. The French and Australian Opens are among the most important events in the world of tennis.

The Olympics

Morocco proudly takes its place among the nations of the world when the Olympics are held, but in 1984 it had something very special to cheer about. That year, in Los Angeles, Nawal el Moutawakel Bennis became the first Moroccan to win an Olympic medal. She won the gold medal in the 400-meter hurdles. This also made her the first woman from any Islamic nation to win a medal. In recognition of this great achievement, she was named to the International Olympic

Committee at the 1998 Olympic Games in Nagano, Japan. She was the first woman from an Islamic nation to be granted this honor.

Road Rally

Once a year, the spectacle of the Paris–Dakar road rally comes roaring through Morocco. This grueling event is a race against time and some of the most difficult road conditions in the world. The contestants can ride in almost anything they want, and they are judged against others in their own class—car, motorcycle, you name it. The race starts in Paris, France, comes south through Europe, and then leaps across the Mediterranean (by ferry), reaching Morocco. It travels through Morocco in stages all the way to the Sahara. From there, it continues south to the city of Dakar in Senegal. The race used to go through Algeria but because of the violence in that country, it now runs the length of Morocco instead.

A contestant bogged down in sand in the Paris–Dakar road rally

Forbidden Images

The Koran forbids the use of images of people or animals. This was intended to prevent people from creating idols and worshiping other gods. This simple restriction has had a powerful impact on the look of objects made in the Muslim world. Denied the use of human or animal images, decoration in the Muslim world often takes the form of geometric elements that are repeated over and over again to form a pleasing design. Designers may use calligraphy, which is the way Arabic script is written.

Because many people read only the Koran, portions of Koranic script are often used as decoration on buildings. These beautiful, curved forms are seen everywhere, on the outside

Koranic script is part of the decoration of this medersa in Fez.

and inside of buildings in Morocco. They are massed on surfaces until they merge into very powerful images. The repetition is never boring; instead, it allows the individual symbol to be seen in two very different ways. First, it may be seen as part of the whole surface; then with a closer look, the element may be seen on its own. It invites calm, serious thought, and an appreciation of the religion. This is a great contrast to the busy, noisy life of the medina.

A World of Contrasts   **113**

Moroccan Arts and Antiquities in Tangier

The history of Morocco's traditional crafts may be seen in Tangier, at the beautiful building that houses the Museum of Moroccan Arts. This ancient building, the Dar el Makhzen, dominates the kasbah of Tangier. It was built in the seventeenth century and was once the governor's palace. The museum occupies part of the building and is as elegant and beautifully decorated as the objects it contains. The floor of the courtyard is laid out in stones that look woven together. Inside are works of art from the entire country, each area represented by art that is typical of the region. Firearms with inlaid designs and beautiful pottery represent the north. Rabat contributes magnificent carpets glowing with rich colors and intricate patterns. The Fez room is dedicated to manuscripts that illustrate the best examples of calligraphy as well as ancient plates that still glow with brilliant colors.

In the same building, the Museum of Antiquities brings Morocco's ancient past to life. All the layers of the civilizations that have come together to create the nation of Morocco are on view, including the Roman sites. The centerpiece of the exhibit on Volubilis is *The Voyage of Venus*, a great mosaic that shows a scene from mythology.

Patterns and Symbols

Whether it's carpets or jewelry, similar intricate patterns make up the design. Moroccan jewelry, both Arabic and Berber, features intricate designs in either silver or gold. Berber designs, however, include symbols that are distinctly non-Muslim. The eye of the partridge is considered very important, a way to ward off evil. The symbol is often styled in such a way that it becomes more of a pattern and less the eye of a real bird. One of the oldest symbols is a small group of diamond shapes that represent a lion's paw.

The symbol of the hand, known as the *khamsa*, is seen everywhere. Small silver khamsas are used on jewelry and painted examples are found on buildings. The symbol is thought to represent the hand of Fatima, the daughter of the prophet Muhammad. It is used to ward off the "evil eye," anything that causes trouble. It's a very powerful symbol in Morocco.

Arts and Crafts

The arts and crafts of Morocco reflect the constant flow of people through the region and through the millennia. By looking closely at the rich imagery of Moroccan rugs, brass objects, and architecture, we can trace this ebb and flow, this tide of cultural influences. In these objects we can read the history of the region. The handicrafts of Morocco's people are easily matched with the area where they are made and with the people who made them. Although the Arab and Berber cultures of Morocco overlap in many ways, the crafts made by

A metalsmith working on a lantern

each group are quite distinct. Arab crafts are generally made by men, who pass their knowledge along from father to son. Berber crafts are made exclusively by women, who pass their heritage along from mother to daughter. But the Berber crafts are fast disappearing as the younger people grow impatient with the lifestyle of their parents.

Carpets

A display of Moroccan carpets

Moroccan carpets are made in both cities and rural areas. In the cities, they are woven by Arab men. In the mountains and the desert areas, Berber carpets are woven by women. Both are well known for their intricate patterns and colors. Working on the simplest of looms, the weavers create complicated and beautiful patterns through the use of different colors. The carpets reflect patterns used by different tribal groups and thus identify the regions in which they were made.

Traditional carpets are made with natural colors from vegetable dyes. The natural colors of the wool—white, beige, and brown—are also used just as they occur. Carpets are made by knotting the yarns around one another. A very fine knotted carpet could have more than 100,000 knots in 10.8 square feet (1 sq m) of carpeting. These carpets are very rare and very expensive because they take so much time to make. But even a carpet of the simplest design and weave takes a great deal of time to make by hand.

Berber Crafts

Berber women traditionally wove everything they wore, as well as the carpets used in the household. They began by making their own yarn from their herds of sheep. The fibers had to be carded, or combed, and then spun into yarn. The yarn was used as it came from the sheep in tones of cream and brown, or it was dyed using natural dyes—red from the pomegranate fruit, blue from indigo, or yellow from saffron. The weaving was done on a simple loom made of sticks. Today, some women use commercial dyes, which are brighter and appeal to certain tourists. Berber carpets are rarely found for sale in the United States. Those that are exported usually go to France. Many are sold directly to tourists in the markets of Morocco.

Opposite: **A Berber woman spinning wool**

In some areas, Berber women even wove the fabric for the tents their families lived in. Some women still weave the *burnous*, a large cloak worn by men. They also weave the *hendira*, a woolen blanket that is worn in place of a coat. It is woven with stripes that indicate the region where it was made. Four or six groups, with a dozen families in each, form a village. Several villages are grouped within the same valley and, together, these form one of the Berber tribes. Each tribe uses a distinctive striped pattern in its weavings.

Modern Dress

In town, men often wear a *djellaba* over their Western clothes. This woven garment is made with an opening for the head. It covers the body from the head to the ankles, and usually has an attached hood. Muslim women in the cities often wear a type of loose-fitting djellaba over their clothes when they go out. It provides a convenient cover-up and, combined with a veil across the face, makes the woman quite unrecognizable. When she returns home, she removes the djellaba. The veil is a piece of fabric that fastens to her head covering.

The changing attitude toward the veil is one of the most dramatic examples of the changes taking place in Morocco. Fewer women are seen wearing the veil today, and those who do wear a veil are generally older women who grew up in a more traditional time. Younger women have created a wide mix of outfits that show a society undergoing change. Some younger women dress in the most modern clothing, even wearing short skirts. Others, who are more observant of Islamic traditions, prefer a more modest outfit consisting of a pair of loose-fitting trousers, a long-sleeved blouse with a high collar, and a closely fitting head scarf. They do not wear the veil.

Young Arab women in Fez

Shifting Sands of Daily Life

The medinas of the old cities exist side by side with modern office buildings. The people who work in those two different areas experience completely different kinds of lives. In the countryside, donkeys carry people along roads where automobiles zip by— two different centuries traveling the same road but at very different speeds. That is life in Morocco today.

F OR THOSE WHO LIVE IN THE CITIES, CHANGE IS EVERYWHERE but always in the midst of tradition. Within the same family, some women choose to wear the veil while others wear Western clothes. Younger, better-educated couples are having fewer children and it is hoped that Morocco's high birthrate and high unemployment will be brought under control in another generation.

Opposite: **Traffic flows past the medina in Marrakesh.**

Mint Tea

Moroccan mint tea is a part of every meal. It is usually served from a silver teapot and poured into small glasses. The art of pouring the tea is part of the pleasure of drinking it. The tea is always poured from a great distance above the glass, as much as 2 feet (61 cm), and it always finds its way to the target. Mint tea is sweetened in the pot before it is served. The fresh mint balances the sugar and makes it a perfect combination. Merchants in shops often offer potential customers a glass of mint tea while they are thinking about their purchases.

Tajine and Couscous

The combination of French and Arabic cooking has given Morocco a delicious cuisine. Spices are at the heart of almost every dish. Moroccan cooks use cinnamon, cumin, coriander, saffron, sesame, and cloves to create tasty stews, meat dishes, and sweets.

The most traditional dish is a *tajine*, named for the covered earthenware dish it is cooked in. The dish has a cone-shaped cover. A tajine may be made with lamb, chicken, or other meat, and is a combination of sweet and sour flavors. A tajine usually includes prunes, almonds, onions, and cinnamon. It is cooked slowly to allow all the flavors to combine. The best tajines are usually those made at home. Although there are cattle in Morocco, the meat is too expensive for most people and has not come into general use. They don't keep pigs because the Koran forbids eating pork. So most meat dishes use lamb, or mutton, which is widely available. Pigeons are often included in dishes, particularly the *pastilla* (*b'stila* in Arabic), a delicious flaky pastry filled with meat, nuts, and spices and coated with sugar and cinnamon before it is baked.

A meal often includes a plate of *couscous*, a fine grain that provides a base for many other dishes. Couscous, a Berber word, is a grain dish made of semolina. The grain is finely ground before it is cooked. Couscous is often served with chicken, lamb, or seafood, along with a variety of vegetables. The grain has the same role in Moroccan cooking that rice has in Chinese food.

A thousand years of tradition is little competition for the riches that seem to be available outside the country. It is not only the lack of jobs that sends Moroccans into Europe looking for work. It is all the foreign visitors who flock to the country and who make their way into every little nook and cranny. To Moroccans, these people represent their countries, and what they see are wealthy people, well dressed and very clean. They think that everyone from those countries must be just like them. It is only when they travel to other countries that they discover there are many, many poor people there too, also looking for work.

Language continues to be at the heart of Morocco's ever-changing culture. Families who speak only Arabic at home may still want their children to speak French in order to take advantage of business opportunities. Those children will be sent to French schools in Morocco. The Moroccan schools are putting a greater emphasis on Arabic and introduce French only at the high school level. Many children leave school before that time. The shortage of primary school places in Morocco has led the government to change its rules about private schools. In the past, it would not accept the certificate earned at a private school. Now it does, because it cannot provide enough

National Holidays in Morocco

January 1	New Year's Day
January 11	Independence Manifesto
March 3	Throne Day
May 1	May Day
May 23	National Day
July 9	Young People's Day
August 14	Allegiance of Wadi-Eddahab
August 20	Anniversary of the King's and People's Revolution
November 6	Anniversary of the Green March
November 18	Independence Day

Religious holidays include Aid el-Fitr, Aid el-Adha, First of Muharram (Muslim New Year), and Milad an-Nabi.

space at existing schools for the flood of children coming into the school system.

Perhaps the biggest change taking place in Morocco is in the home. A man born in 1954 was one of seven children. His father had two wives and was a farmer with little education. But his grandfather had four wives, who had thirty-five children! This man has one wife and two children. And this, he believes, is the future of Morocco.

The king is the best example of how Morocco is trying to maintain its traditions and yet adapt to more modern ways. King Hassan II has proclaimed that a man who wants to marry a second wife, which is allowed under Islam, must have the permission of his first wife.

In the cities, women are entering the modern areas of life but they are often resented by the men who believe they are taking away "men's" jobs. One young woman, Bashara Blaoui, runs a wholesale crafts business in the medina in Marrakesh. She decided to learn English because she felt it would be important in a business in which she deals with many foreigners. Although she is quite independent during her

A young Moroccan businesswoman

workday, when she leaves the shop, she says, "there are no social opportunities here. The religion [Islam] is the way of life. I am one of four sisters and none of them wanted to marry because they did not want to have a Muslim way of life." That meant a life tied to the home. Bashara sees foreign women traveling on their own, or with a friend, and she wishes she could do the same. In order to fit into the life in the medina, where she works, she has created a kind of uniform—a modest pantsuit in a dark color.

A woman in the mountains carrying twigs and leaves for fuel

In the villages and in the medinas, women's roles are very much the same. Their lives are a round of daily chores, cooking, and looking after their children. Women in the mountains wash their clothes in streams and carry wood for cooking fires. Their daughters and their sons want something more. They want the life they see around them when visitors pass through. They know that these visitors don't spend their days hauling wood for fires or plowing a field behind a donkey. Girls are emerging from the home to live a modern life. Women can be found in the army today. Women can be seen in offices. They dress in Western clothes, although they may add a head scarf because they are still tied to Islam. They drive their own cars; they are equal partners with their husbands. All of these different kinds of lives add up to the Morocco of the twenty-first century.

Timeline

Moroccan History		World History	
		c. 2500 B.C.	Egyptians build the Pyramids and Sphinx in Giza.
Phoenicians establish trading posts on the Mediterranean.	12th century B.C.		
		563 B.C.	Buddha is born in India.
Rome begins to dominate the region.	2nd century B.C.		
Northern portion of what is now Morocco becomes part of Roman Empire.	A.D. 42	A.D. 313	The Roman emperor Constantine recognizes Christianity.
		610	The prophet Muhammad begins preaching a new religion called Islam.
Arabs invade Morocco and end Byzantine rule.	682		
Idrisid dynasty rules Morocco, the first Arab rulers to do so.	789–926		
Almoravids rule.	1062–1147	1054	The Eastern (Orthodox) and Western (Roman) Churches break apart.
		1066	William the Conqueror defeats the English in the Battle of Hastings.
		1095	Pope Urban II proclaims the First Crusade.
Almohads rule; Morocco becomes the center of an empire that includes modern-day Algeria, Tunisia, Libya, and large areas of Spain and Portugal.	1147–1258		
Battle of Las Navas de Tolosa, in which Spain defeats the Moroccans. Almohad Empire begins to disintegrate.	1212	1215	King John seals the Magna Carta.
		1300s	The Renaissance begins in Italy.

Moroccan History

Portugal captures the port of Ceuta, beginning Portuguese and Spanish influence in Morocco.	**1415**
The Saadians bring revival to Morocco.	**1554– 1660**
Reign of Ahmed I al-Man-sur; influx of Moors and Jews expelled from Spain after 1492.	**1579– 1603**
The Alawite dynasty succeeds the Saadians.	**1660**
Spain invades Morocco and acquires Tètouan.	**1859– 1860**
Germans support Moroccan resistance to France.	**1911**
France obtains a larger share of Moroccan territory.	**1912**
Abd al Krim organizes a revolt that drives Spanish forces from Moroccan territory.	**1920– 1924**
Morocco achieves peace.	**1934**
Morocco becomes a major Allied supply base.	**1942– 1945**
Sultan Mohammed V is deposed.	**1953**
Morocco gains independence.	**1956**
King Mohammed V dies.	**1961**
Morocco invades Spanish Sahara.	**1975**

World History

1347	The Black Death sweeps through Europe.
1453	Ottoman Turks capture Constantinople, conquering the Byzantine Empire.
1492	Columbus arrives in North America.
1500s	The Reformation leads to the birth of Protestantism.
1776	The Declaration of Independence is signed.
1789	The French Revolution begins.
1865	The American Civil War ends.
1914	World War I breaks out.
1917	The Bolshevik Revolution brings Communism to Russia.
1929	Worldwide economic depression begins.
1939	World War II begins, following the German invasion of Poland.
1957	The Vietnam War starts.
1989	The Berlin Wall is torn down, as Communism crumbles in Eastern Europe.
1996	Bill Clinton re-elected U.S. president.

Fast Facts

Official name: Kingdom of Morocco
(Arabic: *Al-Mamlakah al-Maghribiyah*)

Capital: Rabat

Moulay Idriss

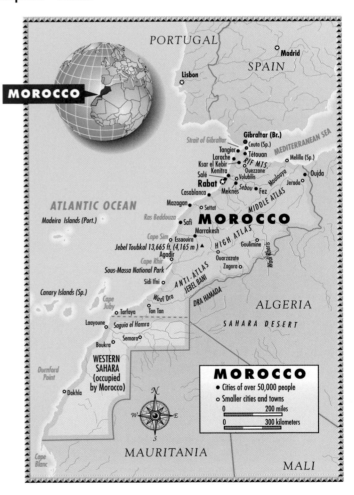

Flag of Morocco

A medersa in Fez

Official language:	Arabic
Official religion:	Islam
National anthem:	"Al Nachid Al Watani" ("The National Anthem")
Government:	Constitutional monarchy
Chief of state:	King
Head of government:	Prime minister
Area:	274,152 square miles (710,000 sq km); includes Western Sahara
Latitude and longitude of geographic center:	32° 00' N, 5° 00' W
Bordering countries:	Morocco (including Western Sahara) shares 1,011 miles (1,627 km) with Algeria; 1,561 miles (2,512 km) with Mauritania; 4 miles (6.4 km) with Spain (Ceuta); and 6 miles (9.6 km) with Spain (Melilla).
Highest elevation:	Jebel Toubkal, 13,671 feet (4,167 m)
Lowest elevation:	Sebkha Tah, 180 feet (55 m) below sea level
Average temperatures:	High: 64–82°F (18–28°C) Low: 46–63°F (8–17° C)

Average annual precipitation:

Tangier	37.5 inches (95 cm)
Casablanca	17 inches (43 cm)
Sahara Desert	less than 4 inches (10 cm)

National population (1997 est.): 30,391,423

Djemaa el Fna

A phosphate plant

50 dirhams

Population of largest cities (1990 est.):

Casablanca	3,210,000
Marrakesh	1,517,000
Rabat	1,472,000
Fez	1,012,000
Tangier	554,000

Famous landmarks:

▶ *In Rabat:* Mohammed V University (1957); the National Conservatory of Music, Dance, and Dramatic Arts; Museum of Moroccan Art; 12th-century Hassan Tower and other parts of the mosque of Yakub al-Mansur (1160–99). Early Christian catacombs are beneath the town, and there are several cave churches and medieval churches and monasteries.

▶ *In Marrakesh:* The medina; Place Djemaa el Fna; 12th-century Koutoubia Mosque with its 220-foot (67-m) minaret; 16th-century Saadi Mausoleum; 18th-century Dar el-BeÔda Palace (now a hospital); 19th-century Bahia royal residence; Menara olive grove; walled, 1,000-acre (405-hectare) Agdal gardens.

▶ *In Tètouan:* The Archaeological Museum has collections of Carthaginian, Roman, and Islamic art and artifacts.

Industry: Phosphate rock mining and processing, food processing, textiles, construction, tourism

Currency: Moroccan dirham (DH); 1999 exchange rate: U.S.$1=9.50 DH

Weights and measures: Metric system

Literacy rate: About 50%

University students

King Hassan II

Common Arabic words and phrases:

Hello	*as-salaam 'alaykum*
Hello (in return)	*wa 'alaykum as-salaam*
Goodbye	*ma' as-salaama*
Good morning	*sabah al-kher*
Good morning (in response)	*sabah an-nur*
Thank you	*shukran (jazilan)*
You're welcome	*la shukran 'ala wajib*
Excuse me	*smeh leeya*
How are you?	*kayf halaalek?*
I don't understand	*ma fhemtesh*
What's your name?	*'eyyet al-bolis?*
I am from America	*ana hna min amreeka*
What is the time?	*sa' a kam?*

Famous Moroccans:

Hassan II *King*	(1930–)
Mohammed Ben Youssef (Mohammed V) *Sultan and king*	(1909–1961)
Ibn Battuta *Traveler and writer*	(1304–?)
Fatima Mernissi *Writer*	(1940–)
Tahar Ben Jelloun *Writer*	(1944–)
Nawal el Moutawakel Bennis *Olympic gold medalist*	(1962–)

To Find Out More

Books

- Bidwell, Margaret, and Robin Bidwell. *Morocco: The Traveller's Companion*. London: I. B. Taurus, 1992; distributed by St. Martin's Press, New York.

- Chottin, Ariane, Catherine Fouré, and Soraya Khalidy, eds. *Morocco*. New York: Alfred A. Knopf, 1996.

- Cross, Mary. *Morocco: Sahara to the Sea*. New York: Abbeville Press, 1995.

- Fernea, Elizabeth Warnock. *A Street in Marrakech*. New York: Doubleday & Co., 1975.

- Gordon, Frances L. et al., eds. *Morocco*. Oakland, Calif.: Lonely Planet, 1997.

- Hargraves, Orin. *Culture Shock: A Guide to Customs and Etiquette*. Singapore: Times Editions, 1995.

- Lerner Publications, Department of Geography Staff, eds. *Morocco in Pictures*. Minneapolis: Lerner Group, 1988.

- Seward, Pat. *Cultures of the World: Morocco*. Tarrytown, N.Y.: Benchmark, 1995.

- Wilkins, Frances. *Morocco*. Broomall, Pa.: Chelsea House, 1988.

Websites

▶ **ArabicNews.com**
www.arabicnews.com
*News, background information,
recipes, and more on Arabic countries
including Morocco*

▶ **CIA World Factbook**
http://www.odci.gov/cia/publications/
factbook/mo.html
*An excellent overview of the
geography, government, and
economy of Morocco*

Embassies and Organizations

▶ **Embassy of the Kingdom
of Morocco**
1601 21st Street, N.W.
Washington, DC 20009
(202) 462-7979

▶ **Moroccan National Tourist Office**
20 East 46th Street
New York, NY 10017
(212) 557-2520

Index

Page numbers in *italics* indicate illustrations

Meet the Authors

Ettagale Blauer first saw Morocco in 1969 on a trip that also took her to neighboring Spain and Portugal. Seeing the cultural connections in the south of Europe and the north of Morocco helped her understand Morocco's rich history. Since then she has been back several times, exploring different parts of the country. "The colors, the smells, the designs that are everywhere in the medinas of Fez and Marrakesh are like nowhere else I've traveled. The change in cultural history is right there—the French are gone, the Africans are far to the south. This is a unique expression of a culture that is truly Arabic. Walking through the medina, at first it's very confusing, but when you take the time to sort it out, you can see that it's all quite well organized." On her most recent trip, she had a henna design painted on her hand and watched in fascination as the woman doing the henna created a design from her head. "I can understand why this is done for special occasions—each time you glance at your hand, you're reminded of your culture."

Jason Lauré's first trip to Morocco was to the charming city of Essaouira, a haven for young travelers. He has explored all the way south, to what was then the Spanish Sahara. He remembers spending days on a road that hardly existed. The new road in the Western Sahara is the visible expression of the changes that have taken place in the country since then. His favorite city is Marrakesh, the gateway to Africa. "When you're in Marrakesh you can feel the Sahara just over the mountains. It's the best example of Morocco's culture. I like the atmosphere and the people. When you're standing in Djemaa el Fna, in the swirl of people, that's really Morocco." On his most recent trip, in 1998, he noted that most of Morocco looks very much the way it did more than twenty years ago. It was a reminder of the country's stability but also of the long path it has to take.

Photo Credits

Photographs ©:

AKG London: 50 bottom (Paul Almasy);
Animals Animals: 31 right (Earth Scenes/Leonard Lee Rue III), 31 left (A. & M. Shah);
AP/Wide World Photos: 54, 56, 62;
Archive Photos: 50 top;
Art Resource, NY: 40 (Erich Lessing), 46 (Snark);
Bridgeman Art Library International Ltd., London/New York: 15 (Delacroix. *A Moroccan Saddling a Horse.* Hermitage, St. Petersburg);
Corbis-Bettmann: 12, 65, 112, 133 bottom (Agence France Presse), 81 (George Kleiman), 48, 51, 52, 57, 61 (UPI), 43, 49;
e.t. archive: 67, 94;
Envision: 124 (Steven Needham);
Gamma-Liaison, Inc.: 68 (D. Benyatouille), 25, 91 (Hulton Getty), 23 (Kurgan-Lisnet), spine (Richard Pasley), 110 (Photo News), 33, 35, 109 (Cecile Treal), 97 (Gabrielle Treal), 8 (Treal-Ruiz);
H. Armstrong Roberts, Inc.: 29 top (Koene);
Lauré Communications: 108 (Ettagale Blauer), 7 top, 20, 76, 82, 85, 87, 90, 101, 122, 126, 132 bottom (Jason Lauré);

Magnum Photos: 107 (Abbas);
National Geographic Image Collection: 18 (Thomas J. Abercrombie), 96 top (James L. Stanfield);
Panos Pictures: 32 (Jean-Leo Dugast), 22 (Alan Le Garsmeur), 127 (Mark McEvoy), 79 top (J. H. Morris);
Peter Arnold Inc.: 13 (Altitude/ Y. Arthus-B.);
Photo Researchers: 70 (Carl Frank), 24, 72 top, 132 center (Noboru Komine), 74 (Paul Stepan), 29 bottom (Roger Wilmshurst);
Photri: 41, 45, 114, 130;
Robert Fried Photography: 7 bottom (Sophie Dauwe), 2, 11, 75, 88 top, 88 bottom, 93, 96 bottom, 99, 102, 116, 121, 123, 133 top;
Robert Holmes Photography: cover, 6, 27, 64, 69, 72 bottom, 84;
Tony Stone Images: 113, 131 (Glen Allison), 105 (John Beatty), 98 (Gerard Del Vecchio), 117 (Robert Everts), 28, 38, 79 bottom (Robert Frerck), 77, 132 top (Sylvain Grandadam), 9, 36 (Steve Vidler);
Victor Englebert: 14, 21, 71, 78, 83, 92, 106, 119;
Visuals Unlimited: 30 (Gerald Corsi).

Maps by Joe LeMonnier